SUPER-HUMAN PERFORMANCE II

SUPER-HUMAN PERFORMANCE II

UTILIZING YOUR GIFTS TO PERFORM AT EXTRAORDINARY LEVELS

DARRAYL & DERRICK MILES

MILESTONE
PUBLISHING HOUSE

Library of Congress Control Number: 2010913135
International Standard Book Number: 978-0-9828393-4-8
E-book ISBN: 978-0-9828393-8-6

First Edition

11 12 13 14 15 — 9 8 7 6 5 4 3 2 1

Printed in Canada

DEDICATION

This book is dedicated to the billions of people world-wide that have a unique Gift to complete their ultimate assignment on earth. It is our hope that this book series encourages us to learn our Gifts and strategically apply those Gifts to improve the lives of others.

CONTENTS

THE GIFT OF GIVING IN ACTION

Darrayl and Derrick Miles are exercising their Gift of Giving by donating 10% of all proceeds of the Superhuman Performance® franchise to two of their favorite charities:

- Metro Hope For Kids Project

- Orlando Magic Youth Foundation

If you believe in helping our children reach their maximum potential; please consider a donation.

■ ■

ORLANDO MAGIC YOUTH FOUNDATION
WHERE YOU MAKE THE DIFFERENCE.

ORLANDO MAGIC YOUTH FOUNDATION

There is no doubt that children—their dreams, their hopes and their potential—represent our future. From educational and arts programs to health programs focused on preventing childhood obesity, the Orlando Magic Youth Foundation is dedicated to nourishing the minds and bodies of children that need it most. Over the last 21 years, the OMYF has distributed more than $16 million to local non-profit community organizations.

The OMYF raises community dollars annually through donations, auctions and events such as the Black Tie and Tennies Gala and the OMYF Open Golf Tournament. With administrative costs covered, 100% of your gift goes directly to benefit children. Plus the McCormick Foundation provides a $.50 match to make your donation go even further!

Make your difference today by donating at **omyf.org**.

METRO HOPE FOR KIDS

Out of the pain, impoverishment and isolation of his own abandonment, Bill Wilson established Metro Ministries in 1980 in what was one of Brooklyn's roughest neighborhoods. Over the years, he has developed a heart of compassion for suffering children everywhere. From the ghettos of America to the townships of South Africa, villages of Eastern Europe, slums of India and islands of the Philippines, he has rescued hurting children and given them hope for the future. Every week 40,000 children in these countries are being touched with love.

With a mandate to help, I'm looking for ordinary people with extraordinary hearts who are willing to give of their time, talents and finances. I need your help to change an old, condemned hospital in Brooklyn, NY, into a community food-and-clothing pantry, as well as a place to hold after-school programs for boys and girls, mentoring programs for youth, and adult programs to help men and women who are coming out of drug addiction. Will you say yes and join a team that makes a difference?

For more information or to give to Metro Hope For Kids, go to www.metrohopeforkids.org. Your donations will change possibilities into realities for boys and girls around the world. Thank you for being one who makes a difference in the life of a child!

—Rosella Angel Ridings, Founder

Introduction

It is my prayer that you have had the wonderful experience of discovering the impact of the first seven gifts covered in *Superhuman Performance* (Administration, Craftsmanship, Discernment, Faith, Giving, Knowledge, and Writing). *Superhuman Performance II* helps you to understand and experience the next level. What's the next level? I'm glad you asked! The next level is when your gift makes room for you and people begin to seek you out to give you the opportunity to utilize your gift every day, regardless of your station in life. You can be at the so-called bottom of society or in the middle of a career change, you can even feel like you were dealt a bad hand in life. But your gift will still make room for you. When it does, when you reach the next level by utilizing your gift daily, you will feel you're leading a life of joy, fulfillment, and purpose!

Let me give a real life example. In January, 2011, a panhandler named Ted Williams made international news when his Gift was discovered on a slow news day in Columbus, Ohio. People from all over the world were enamored with his Gift. Here was a gentleman in tattered clothing with hair that appeared to have been unkept for years. But he believed he had a Gift. His belief was so strong that while begging for change in the middle of an intersection, he held a sign that read "I Have a God-Given Gift of Voice." Because of his belief, one man took notice and recorded an unprofessional video of Ted and uploaded it to

YouTube. Within 48 hours of Ted's Gift being discovered, he experienced the next level. The world began to seek him out so he could utilize his Gift daily. Ted received multiple offers for jobs and appearances on top tier-television programs. Quicken Loans even offered him a free home loan. What I would have liked to have seen in the media frenzy was the message to all people that everyone has a Gift.

I must admit that the Man With the Golden Voice gave me more excitement for this book series. And with Superhuman Performance II, I share that excitement so you might discover your Gifts and begin working within them. For when you do, you will experience the next level. In this book, you will discover seven more Gifts: Compassion, Encouragement, Helps/Serving, Hospitality, Leadership, Teaching, and Wisdom. Some of the people I highlight include Genma Holmes, Pam Boney, Angela Johnson McGee, Elmer Towns, Keith Harrell, Pastor Sunday Adelaja, George C. Fraser, and Roger Andersen. I even give a bonus profile for Alma Rivera. Akin to the "Man With the Golden Voice," several people in this book know what it is like to be disadvantaged, live in a family split because of a mothers illness, be a child walking barefoot amongst trash in a developing country, and go through the life shifts of many career changes. Each story is one of triumph! And triumph came when these individuals recognized the Gifts they had inside of themselves. My hope is that you discover your own Gift and use your Gift to ultimately serve others.

Superhumanly yours,

Darrayl Miles

Gift Preview

Compassion

Compassion is the special gift whereby the Spirit enables certain people to feel exceptional empathy for sufferers, to speak words of compassion, and to care for people with acts of love that help alleviate their distress.

People with this gift:

- Focus on alleviating the sources of pain or discomfort in suffering people.

- Address the needs of the lonely and forgotten.

- Exhibit love, grace, and dignity to those facing hardships and crises.

- Serve in difficult or unsightly circumstances and do so cheerfully.

- Are involved in dissolving individual or social issues that oppress people.

Encouragement

Encouragement is the gift God gives some Christians that enables them to offer comfort, words of encouragement, hope, and reassurance to discouraged, weak, or troubled people in such a way that they are consoled.

People with this gift:

- Come to the side of those who are discouraged to reassure them and give them hope.

- Emphasize God's promises and confidence in His will.

HELPS/SERVING

Helps/Serving is the gift that enables a believer to work gladly behind the scenes so God's work is fulfilled. Service is the special ability that God gives to some Christians that allows them to serve the church in a supporting roll or to invest their talents in the life and ministry of other members of the body, enabling them to increase their effectiveness. It allows certain people to accomplish practical and necessary tasks that support others, ease their burdens, and meet their needs.

People with this gift:

- Serve behind the scenes whenever needed to support the gifts and ministries of others without having to be asked.

- See what needs to be done, and they enjoy doing it.

- Sense God's purpose and take pleasure in meeting everyday responsibilities.

- Attach spiritual value to practical service.

- Enjoy knowing that they are making other people's lives easier by doing what God has called them to do.

- Would rather do a job than find someone else to do it.

HOSPITALITY

Hospitality is the special ability God gives to some people to provide an open home and warm welcome to those in need of food, lodging, and fellowship. It involves a readiness to invite strangers to your home (or church) for the sake of the gospel.

People with this gift:

- Provide an environment where people feel valued and cared for.

- Meet new people and help them to feel welcome.

- Create a safe and comfortable setting where relationships can develop.

- Connect people so they can build meaningful relationships.

- Set people at ease in unfamiliar surroundings.

LEADERSHIP

Leadership is the special ability God gives to some people that enables them to set goals in accordance with God's purpose and to communicate these goals to others in such a way that they voluntarily and harmoniously work together to accomplish these goals for the glory of God.

People with this gift:

- Provide direction for God's people or ministry.
- Motivate others to perform to the best of their abilities.
- Present the "big picture" for others to see.
- Model the values of the ministry.
- Take responsibility and establish goals.

TEACHING

Teaching is the special ability God gives to some people that enables them to clearly explain the truths of God's word and to apply them so that other people understand, learn, and grow.

People with this gift:

- Communicate biblical truth that inspires greater obedience to the Word.

- Challenge listeners simply and practically with the truths of Scripture.

- Focus on changing lives by helping others understand the Bible better.

- Give attention to detail and accuracy.

- Prepare through extended times of study and reflection.

WISDOM

Wisdom is the gift that allows the believer to sort through opinions, facts, and thoughts in order to determine what solution would be best for the individual believer or the community of believers. The ability to apply knowledge to life in such a way as to make spiritual truths quite relevant and practical in proper decision making and daily life situations.

People with this gift:

- Focus on the unseen consequences in determining the next steps to take

- Receive an understanding of what is necessary to meet the needs of the body

- Provide divinely given solutions in the midst of conflict and confusion

- Hear the Spirit provide direction for God's best in a given situation

- Apply spiritual truth in specific and practical ways.

CHAPTER 1

UNCOMMON CUSTOMER SERVICE

Genma Stringer Holmes: If It Moves, Call Genma Stringer Holmes

Do not forget to show hospitality to strangers, for by so doing some people have shown hospitality to angels without knowing it.

—HEBREWS 13:2, NIV

Name: Genma Stringer Holmes
Position: Founder
Companies: Holmes Pest Control and GSH Consulting, LLC
Gift: Hospitality

The bite of the brown recluse spider is extremely painful. Within forty-eight hours, the spider's venom causes the skin to form a rose-colored halo around the base of a purple blister. Next, a scab appears followed by a rash that devours more skin cells, leaving victims with muscle and joint pain.

Chills, headaches, and nausea may follow. If left untreated, the bite can lead to death of the flesh.

So how did an attractive and buoyant African American model with an aversion to creepy-crawly things end up in the pest control business? "The opportunities are endless," says Genma Stringer Holmes. "I followed the money and my passion for people."

Over twenty years ago, Genma's husband was hired by Anheuser Busch as an engineer. His responsibilities included overseeing plant assembly installations. As Genma explains, her husband soon found a nest of problems and a huge opportunity.

"Right away, he ran into problems with rodents that were plaguing plant operations," she says. "Roger being an analytical guy researched how much the company was spending on their pest control budget. When I heard the figures for one plant I said, 'Honey, you're on the wrong side of this coin; you need to be killing the rats. Let somebody else deal with plant operations.' One of the reasons I went from the runway to killing bugs was because of the little-known lucrative opportunities in the pest control industry. If it bugs you, it is money to me."

Genma researched the pest control business and found that owners in her area were making six figures and above. And with few women and even fewer minorities out front, most of the businesses were run my white men. So Genma, with her flair for style, decided she could compete successfully by changing the face of the industry.

"Bugs are a business to me, not an obsession. I'm not the pest control owner who sits and holds a bug in my hand for hours examining it. That's not me. But I know this industry inside and out, and I'm always learning more. I research and study everything I can get my hands on about my industry. My thirst for knowledge is insatiable. Learning never gets old in this business. But no matter how much I've studied I have not overcome my fear of spiders. Yes, I know it's perplexing. You put me in a room with spiders, and I'll come unglued. The brown recluse is my worst nightmare. They are mean and vicious. They cause serious harm, and the scars are disfiguring. Here I am Miss Vanity that cannot live without skin lotions and body treatments, and I'm hunting down these venomous spiders that can mutilate my skin tissue. For me to be in the pest control business and be successful at what I do daily, it's totally a God thing."

A Different Kind of Businesswoman

When it comes to business, Genma is old school. She focuses on friends, fellowship, and good food, the trademark of someone with the gift of hospitality.

"I remember being a child standing on the porch and waving at strangers, calling to them to come into our home. My grandmother would say, 'Girl, shut your mouth! What's the matter with you talking to people you don't know?' But that was how God had made me. Later, as I became a student of the Word, I understood that what I'd been given was the gift of hospitality. Hugs and hellos are second nature to me.

"Unfortunately, I don't see a lot of hospitality in today's marketplace. Instead, pushy, rude, greedy business owners are looking out for themselves rather than their customers. How sad. When I travel, I often stay at someone's home instead of a hotel. With the rise in bed bugs at hotels, do you blame me? By staying in a customer's home, I get to sit down and talk to them one-on-one, and we get to know each other better. And when I get the precious opportunity to be a visitor, I am always willing to cook a big southern meal—a small token of my gratitude for having someone's home opened to me."

Food, fellowship, and loyalty to her clients are the keys to Genma's success. This is true for her pest control business and her marketing firm GSH Consulting.

"I can only recall a few times where I entered into a contract with someone without first breaking bread with them," she says. "I believe strongly my customers are family and in order for me to get to know someone well enough to be part of my family, we need to sit down and share a meal together. On the first outing with potential clients, I take them to lunch or dinner. But if it's a serious relationship, breakfast is a must.

"In Tennessee, everyone knows that real business is done before 8:00 AM. Breakfast is considered the power meal of the day. A breakfast appointment signals to others that you are an early riser and you are starting your day determined and focused. Once I asked a billionaire to mentor me, and he asked me if I was willing to meet for breakfast. I naturally said, 'Yes, sir.' Years later, he told me that I would never have gotten the chance to shadow him if I was not willing to get up early to meet with him and his team.

"Jesus rose early in the morning to spend time with his Father. For relationships that are important and special, investing in early morning outings is the key to being grounded and successful. That's huge. When someone agrees to eat with me, I cherish that time because it's their time. They're giving of themselves.

"My biggest business expense is eating out. One restaurant in particular gets about $300 a month by serving as a venue for me to entertain breakfast guests. This relationship has become one of my biggest referral sources. Last month, I spent $289 on breakfast and $749 on dinner. In return, the restaurant referred nine customers to me. Those nine referrals netted me $50,000 in business.

"There are a lot of business people who just want to get through a meal in a hurry. They're not really there for the person but for the business that person represents. That's what I call 'a quickie.' Too often, we forget that we're dealing with people, not products, and the reason we're here is to glorify God in all that we do. Often, we don't stop to think that as business owners we need to serve others."

More evidence of Genma's old school business philosophy is her commitment to a printed newsletter for her clients. In each edition of "The Pest Gazette," Genma publicizes her clients' good news. New babies, engagements, and graduations are all reasons for celebration and inclusion in "The Pest Gazette."

"Once I started sharing my family news and accomplishments with my customers, everyone started telling me about their family's good news. 'Mrs. Holmes, do not forget to mention my grand-baby in your newsletter.' We live in the age of social media and e-zines, but my customers tell me they still love the printed newsletter. They like to read without being bombarded by e-mails and Facebook notifications. People who've been long-time subscribers to my newsletter remember when my youngest son won the state championship in little league football. A few years later when he won a high school championship, they reminded me of his earlier success. That was special for my young son. When folks can remember your children's football games, that's being more than a customer to me. That is family love. A printed newsletter mailed to a home address tells your clients you're fully invested in them. Printing and shipping adds costs to communicating your marketing message, but it's worth it. You're telling your customers they are significant to you and you want to include them in your life."

> They devoted themselves to the apostles' teaching and to fellowship, to the breaking of bread and to prayer. (Acts 2:42 NIV)

For Genma, networking is more than handing out business cards at chamber events. It's about building a net of relationships reinforced by folks who have your back. "Networking is a not seeing how many business cards you can collect in one night. That's pan handling. Real networking is helping others. For example, I'm in a networking group that meets twice a month. At each meeting, we have sixty seconds to plug our businesses. Now for many people this would be the time to tell everything about their business, product, or service. But in this group, we understand that networking isn't about what you advertise; it's about what you give to others in sixty seconds. One member in our group sold Donald Trump's Trump Tower. He's a commercial real estate broker. Rarely have I heard him announce at our meetings what properties he has for sale. Instead, he uses his time to thank the people in the room who've recently helped him land a deal or introduced him to a new client. He spends his time praising others and telling stories about deals that involve members in the group. He leaves our meetings with everyone else falling over themselves to refer him to their clients and everyone else they meet. True networking is building a network of people working for you."

Friend-to-Friend Referrals

Genma believes (and most studies concur) the best customer is a word-of-mouth customer. "Nothing is greater than having a friend referred to me for business. By the time I speak to a referral, he or she has been told everything about me. Usually before I finish my greetings, they're repeating my life story back to me. And by the time we begin to talk about their pest problems, I already know a bit about them because they've been pre-qualified by the client who referred them to me. When I invest time in friends who make referrals, barriers are removed. Selling is done before I meet potential customers. So in most cases, I only need to close the deal.

"With Yellow Pages shoppers, I'm only a business with a short description of services that my company provides. That's not a relationship. I rarely get more than five or six custom-ers a month from the Yellow Pages. And most of those aren't long-term clients. They're not looking for an ongoing relation-ship with a pest service provider. When I finish the job, they're gone. But a new customer who is a friend of a friend, someone I have met and spent time getting to know, will become a long-term client and, most importantly, will tell others about my business."

Get Involved in the Community

Genma participates in many charity events in her area and believes strongly in the adage, *To whom much is given, much is required.* She also believes it resonates within the busi-ness community.

"When folks meet me at fundraisers or see my company has donated items to their kids' little league sports, that's advertis-ing for my business. When my son played football, I had a big sign in the stadium supporting his team. I rather spend money marketing little league sports than put money into ads for the Yellow Pages. I invest my money in people and organizations that help the youth succeed."

Quest for Success

"Many business owners are successful on the outside and a mess on the inside," Genma says. "That's how the devil works. He attacks us from the inside out, and your family is the most vulnerable. If you ever want to get me distracted just let something be off balance with my children. I become a mess quickly. But I've learned over the years that one of the greatest gifts we can give our children is to be in prayer for them all the time and not to become distracted by their shenanigans and all that comes with life as young children become young adults. I think as business owners we need to have prayer plans for our families just like we have a business plans for our companies."

Spend Time Lifting Up Somebody Else

Genma contends the main place to use your gift is in the marketplace. That's where people see who you really are, not as you appear on Sunday.

"The person you are on the job or in the office," she says, "is the person people see outside of church, and that's your real testimony. If you go to church three days a week, you still influence more people at your office than you will sitting in a pew. Marketplace Christians are high in demand and needed badly. We need more of us talking less about Christ and imitating his actions more. Start where you are. Simple things like sending a thank you note can have far greater impact on people you encounter daily. Not an e-mail, but a hand written note. Spend your time talking about the goodness of others and building up souls and their businesses. The more we speak well of others, the less time we have to add to a negative toxic environment that can be all-consuming. When we talk about the success of others and less about our own, folks take notice. I've found the above actions have come back to me with interest."

Heart's Desire

> Until we change our attitudes toward how we do business within our race and culture, we will never truly forge ahead.
>
> —Genma Stringer Holmes

No matter what line of work a person is in, Genma believes the individual behind the successful business person really deserves the credit.

"Anytime I meet a couple, I ask, 'Which one is the dreamer and which one just wants to get the bills paid?' In any marriage, relationship, or business, you must have a balance between the two people. In my marriage, I'm definitely the dreamer, and my husband is the practical one. When I go off into dream land, he'll give me time and then pull me back down to earth. But that's a good thing. There was a time when I felt as if I was being suffocated, as if he was trying to kill my spirit and my dreams. But with much prayer and help from others, he came to understand that a dreamer can lead the vision, the dreamer sees the potential of what can be. I had to learn to be sensible about those dreams and goals, and that's where the realist comes in and gives balance. In any relationship, it helps to let the visionary dream and let the realist be realistic. If you don't, strife is inevitable. With two dreamers, you go broke. With two realists, you go nowhere. But if a dreamer and a realist work together, they can go as far as the Lord leads."

Gift Wrap

- Customers are family and in order for me to get to know someone well enough to be part of my family, we need to sit down and break bread

- In Tennessee, everyone knows that real business is done before 8:00 AM. Breakfast is considered the power meal of the day

- When I invest time in friends who make referrals, barriers are removed. Selling is done before I meet potential customers. So in most cases, I only need to close the deal.

Genma's Other Gifts: Giving

CHAPTER 2

WHICH WAY DO YOU TILT?

Pam Boney: The Art of the Transcendent Leader

For we are his workmanship, created in Christ Jesus
for good works, which God prepared beforehand,
that we should walk in them.

—EPHESIANS 2:10, ESV

> Name: Pam Boney
> Position: Founder & CEO
> Company: Tilt 360 Leadership, Inc.
> Gift: Hospitality

The evening should have been the pinnacle of Pam Boney's
career. Hospitality was her profession, making others feel
comfortable, her calling. But as she walked toward the stage,
listening as the chairman of the board lauded her accomplishments, she felt anything but content and relaxed. Her evening
gown was too tight, the heels too high. Pam was a jeans-and-
sneakers sort of leadership executive, and this award ceremony

with its accolades, applause, and formal setting was too restrictive. She wanted to run, to head for the exit. But instead, she paused at the bottom of the steps, listening as her boss recounted her accomplishments.

Pam glanced around the room, smiling at friends, watching as others silently toasted her with flute glasses filled with champagne. A chandelier began to move ever so slightly as a ceiling vent blasted cold air. When her name was called, she stepped onto the stage. Men in tuxedoes stood, clapping. A woman she'd mentored wiped tears from her cheeks. Pam's forceful steps clicked against varnished wood as she approached the podium. Her boss hugged her and placed the trophy in her arms, then backed away. For a moment she stood, alone, blinded by bright lights and the memory of the hours of hard work. Was it real? Had she finally grabbed the brass ring? Then why did her heart hurt so? The crowd lingered, gathering around to congratulate her. She grew tired of holding the trophy, and she sat it on the table. The music stopped. The ball ended.

She returned to her room. Sitting on her bed a few minutes later, she began to make the obligatory calls to her staff members, thanking them for their hard work, their hours of overtime, and their commitment to her vision of success. *What an imposter I am*, she thought. *If this is success, then why am I feeling so sad right now?* On the phone, Pam sounded gracious and sincere while trying to mask the weariness she felt. At last the calls ended. She looked at the phone. *Who next? My daughter is in bed. Too late to call mom and dad. My ex—why would he care? Don't have any friends outside of those I work with. There must be someone else I can share this moment with.*

But there wasn't.

"I sat there in a state of shock," Pam says, reflecting on that evening. "The trajectory of my life flashed through my mind, and I wondered what I'd been so desperate to find, so determined to accomplish. I'd thought that being the best in the business would mean more. I think we all feel that way at times. We set goals and believe if we can just climb one more rung or land one more sale we'll find joy. But in the end it's not what we do that matters or how well we do it; it's the people we touch along the way. Great leaders know this. They understand that mending relationships is the price of survival, and a real friend, someone who knows you inside and out, is the image of God."

Pam took the trophy home to an unfurnished house with dead plants, a half-painted bedroom, and a hallway full of unopened boxes. For years she'd planned to unpack, build a home—build a life. But she'd never found the time. Work was her god. Suddenly the trophy didn't represent victory but loss, brokenness, and abandonment.

"Whatever I thought I'd experience, the euphoria I'd expected to feel —never happened," Pam says. "I discovered there was this wide gap between who I was at work and who I was in my personal life, and in that moment I realized what I wanted more than anything in the world wasn't a trophy to hold but for someone to hold me. I wanted someone to love me not because of what I'd done and could do but because of who

I was. I wanted someone to really see me for who I was—a lost, lonely, and scared little girl who was flying too high."

Ahead of Her Time

Pam experienced a radical shift in her career after that evening. She stopped focusing on the bottom line and began focusing on people. Her staff, the guests, her management team. She shifted her attention away from profit and loss statements and toward the people within her sphere of influence. Since she worked daily with her staff, she decided to make employee satisfaction her number one goal. If she could prove to her employees that she cared about them as individuals, then the profits and performance issues would take care of themselves. For that to happen, however, she would need their help.

"I began collecting data on human behavior patterns and found that what I had valued as a positive trait can actually become harmful when overused. For example, I'm a free-spirited person who tends to be a little too forgiving and compassionate. I know that sounds wrong when I say it that way, but what this means is I sometimes let things slide and give people the benefit of the doubt when I shouldn't. The result is people take advantage of me. As a manager and person I'm too permissive and don't always enforce the rules. The result is a staff that's accustomed to confusion and chaos.

"When I veer to the opposite extreme, however, and become a stickler for the rules, leaving no room for grace and forgiveness, then I come across as judgmental, cold, and uncaring. So the more I studied my own motivations and human behavior in general, the more I came to realize Christ was right. He was the only truly 'whole' person. He could play in all areas of human virtues and do it perfectly. His life was centered and balanced, and as executives, we should strive to follow His model."

> Every road is rough for the man with no friends.
>
> —ANONYMOUS

Tilted in the Right Way

After years of study, testing, and application development, Pam has identified twelve core character strengths that are split into four quadrants: Head, Gut, Spirit, and Heart. If a leader is able to master each quadrant, performance can be exponential instead of incremental. Why? Leaders who can be objective and put the needs of the enterprise above their own interests possess strong character, they are concerned about how their teams impact their communities and virally influence culture. For the sake of time, I'll give insight to the Head and Heart quadrants."

Head Quadrant

"Wisdom is how we generally define someone gifted with good judgment," Pam says. There is a difference between being smart and being wise, and judgment is that difference. An individual with this ability is able to think critically and logically. They display the qualities of perspective, temperance, and diligence. You'll find that a person with perspective is able to quickly distinguish truth from error, right from wrong. This isn't based on feelings but on truth. They'll recognize inconsistencies in policy, documents, and behaviors. Someone with the gift of temperance is able to act with moderation and exercise self-control. They're able to control their emotions. Diligence is the ability to maintain a disciplined mind and focus on what is helpful and productive, instead of what is distorted or destructive.

"The opposite of wisdom is resilience. Someone with a bent toward wisdom sees the world as black and white with neat and tidy rules, but resilient people see the world in color and love to create uncertainty. They're creative, receptive to new ideas, and inspired in ways that others aren't. They can catch a vision, dream dreams, and think outside the box. In fact, that's one reason they butt heads so often with the wisdom crowd. The creative types are almost never in the box. But they're great at coming up with new solutions to entrenched problems.

"If you think of Christ, he was both the fulfillment of the Law and the spirit of God. He was clear that He didn't come to abolish the Law but to complete it, and He did that by both understanding truth, because He is truth, and demonstrating that rules, in themselves, don't save us. But the spirit of the Law is in truth. So when you're able to balance both tendencies of the mind, you can perform at superhuman levels."

Heart Quadrant

> Abundant living begins with friends.
>
> —ANONYMOUS

"A person who plays in the quadrant of 'humanity' tends to focus on people more than problems," Pam says. "They like to form trusting relationships, act diplomatically, and speak with tact. They're compassionate and caring. In the same quadrant, you'll also find people who seek justice. They're courageous, passionate, self-confident, and willing to suffer loss or take risk for the greater good. Whereas the compassionate person might stop to help every wounded soldier, the courageous individual would push on to the final goal regardless of the cost and is quite comfortable taking whatever risk is called for to win the battle. Too much humanity can become permissive and is a perversion of a good thing. Too much courage becomes arrogance, also a perversion of a good thing. The key is to develop all of the virtues and not overuse them, so we can relate to people wherever they are in their spiritual journey.

"I'm convinced the more we aspire to live like Christ with His character qualities and with His ability to transcend Himself for the greater good of others, the more we'll be able to perform at extraordinary levels. This is my mission and ministry as a person with the gift of caring and hospitality. It may very well be that I was born for this very reason."

Gift Wrap

- I came to realize Christ was right. He was the only truly 'whole' person. He could play in all areas of human virtues and do it perfectly. His life was centered and balanced, and as executives, we should strive to follow His model."

- Leaders who can be objective and put the needs of the enterprise above their own interests possess strong character, they are concerned about how their teams impact their communities and virally influence culture.

- There is a difference between being smart and being wise, and judgment is that difference.

Pam's Other Gifts: Leadership

CHAPTER 3

MOVING FROM POWER TO PASSION

Evelyn Neely: Leadership Development One Dream at a Time

And appoint one leader from each tribe to help assign the land.

—NUMBERS 34:18, NIV

Name: Evelyn Neely
Position: Vice President of
Organizational Development
Company: Ryla, Inc.
Gift: Leadership

Have you ever wondered why God chose you for certain opportunities and experiences? Have you ever accomplished something amazing that you had previously thought impossible? Have you ever found yourself comfortable, content, and confident in your abilities, only to be thrust into a challenging situation that far exceeds your skills?

"Moving from power to passion is the natural progression of every successful servant," Evelyn Neely says. "In talks I explain how we are blessed with experiences and positions that we never dreamed possible—and in some cases we'd choose to skip. But ultimately we see that these hurdles, challenges, and mountain-top summit experiences are all part of God's master plan for our lives. I'm firmly convinced that God allows adversity to lead us to success. But it's on His timeline, not ours. When we listen to God, He leads us into the next season of our success."Evelyn's program, Moving from Power to Passion, began when she was asked to deliver a workplace testimony at a prestigious women's conference.

"I knew I had a testimony," she says. "I mean, who works 33 years at a major corporation like Xerox and doesn't? But I wasn't sure what portion of my career would speak to the women in that audience, so I prayed about it until God revealed to me that I should tell people how I voluntarily left a lucrative career at a major corporation in order to join a small but growing company that fueled my passion. I walked away from the power, position, and influence in order to pursue my heart's desire, a desire placed inside of me by God Himself. And I have to tell you, taking that leap of faith was terrifying.

"For years I knew I wanted to help develop leaders. I wanted to make a difference in the lives of the people and give back in the way the Apostle Paul calls us to serve—preach, teach, write. But due to my success as a corporate executive, I never had the chance to really focus on that passion. I think that's why God spoke to me. He led me to Ryla as a consultant.

There I was allowed to operate in my passion, and that's the message I want to deliver to everyone who's in the marketplace, from Wall Street to Main Street. With His help, anyone can move from power to passion. Note, I didn't mention prosperity. Often we sacrifice financially in order to do the thing we're gifted to pursue. But rarely do I find someone who wants to go back to working for just the paycheck. Most are content to lose what they can't keep—job security, for example—in order to gain fulfillment and a legacy."

Evelyn recalls how in the corporate structure she was bound by guidelines, policies, and procedures. "I enjoyed my work at Xerox, I truly did. But there wasn't much room for passion unless it was passion for the bottom line. And that's not a bad thing. But when His Spirit moves within you and gifts you with skills and a calling, then you begin to sense an uneasiness in your soul. In time you just know you're meant to do more. In the company I work for now I can bring my Bible to work, I can pray with people. I can talk with them about the deep issues we all struggle with: loss, pain, failure, and our eternal future. I can coach and counsel in ways I never could when I worked in a corporate setting. I can bring my heart to work, and that makes a huge difference."

The Freedom to Lead

Evelyn has always had the gift of leadership, always felt called to inspire, motivate, and lead by example.

"Of all my strengths, I'd say leadership and discernment are my two greatest gifts. And they're actually well-suited for the type of work required by the marketplace. Without discernment you'll lead people in the wrong direction, but without the gift of leadership you'll know the right course but be unable to affect the necessary change.

"I also have the gifts of teaching and service, but I use my gift of leadership much more, especially in the areas of leadership development. For example, we recently formed an organizational development team focused on training, developing, coaching, and counseling current and potential leaders. This is the first one of those Ryla ever had. We also kicked off a new mentoring program. In both cases those programs are the direct result of our freedom to use our gifts in order to help others."

Dreams Sprout One Individual at a Time

Evelyn urges those who are not ready to pursue their dream to remain faithful and work in the field where they're planted.

"You can still make an impact in the workplace even if you're not pursuing your dream," she says. "In fact, often God allows us to settle and grow in the field in which we're planted in order to test our motives and reach some who we might otherwise never touch.

"For example, when I was promoted to vice president at Xerox, I clearly hadn't asked for the assignment, nor did I want it. But sometimes God gives us tasks we don't want in order to prepare us for the thing we do desire. So I took the position. I didn't feel that I was equipped nor capable of succeeding in that role, but I always knew that God had my back. I knew he would help me overcome any obstacle I faced. And He did. He really touched me through prayer and deepened my faith. There were times when I was so lost that if it wasn't for God's guidance and direction I would have failed gloriously. But each day he helped me accomplish the work placed before me. So my faith, prayer life, and constant contact with God have personally helped me accomplish things that, in the flesh, would have never been possible."

Take Care of Your People

Evelyn has a simple principle for success. Pursue the passion God places in your heart, trust him fully for the results, work as if you're working solely for God, and take care of the people around you.

"In the leadership classes or when I speak to groups of people, I always tell them that if you want to be successful, then you need to take care of your people. If you take care of your people, they will take care of your customers, and that in turn will take care of your business. If you take care of your people, it will make a huge difference in your success."

Blessed to Be Blessed

"When I left Xerox," Evelyn says, "I served in a leadership role at my church for almost two years. That was sort of my down time, my resting in the Lord. But then I felt this yearning to go back into the workplace. So I came to Ryla as a leadership consultant. That was something that had always been a desire of mine. As they began to grow, they asked me to come on board full time as Assistant Vice President of Organizational Development.

"Now you have to understand, and I tell people this all the time, before you can be successful you need to know in what areas you are gifted because many times the areas where you're gifted will lead to financial blessings. Not always, but often that's the case. Understand, you shouldn't work within your gifting solely for the purpose of making money. The gift is from God and is to be used for His glory and to help others. However, often times when you are working within the strength of your gift and in the center of your passion, you will be financially blessed. I would just caution, however, that you should always check your motives to make sure your heart and purpose are pure.

"I've found if you serve in your gifted area you will be a greater blessing to the people whom you serve because you're doing something that you have a passion for. I've also learned that serving and making a difference in other people's lives will bless *you* far more than it will ever bless *them*."

Gift Wrap

- Hurdles, challenges, and mountain-top summit experiences are all part of God's master plan for our lives. I'm firmly convinced that God allows adversity to lead us to success. But it's on His timeline, not ours. When we listen to God, He leads us into the next season of our success.

- Often we sacrifice financially in order to do the thing we're gifted to pursue. But rarely do I find someone who wants to go back to working for just the paycheck. Most are content to lose what they can't keep —job security, for example —in order to gain fulfillment and a legacy.

- Often times when you are working within the strength of your gift and in the center of your passion, you will be financially blessed.

Evelyn's Other Gift: Discernment

CHAPTER 4

LIVE ON THE SET!

Angela Johnson McGee: Cast Into the Perfect Role

He said, "Listen to my words: When prophets are among you, I, the Lord, will show myself to them in visions; I will speak to them in dreams."

—NUMBERS 12:6, NCV

Name: Angela Johnson McGee
Positions: Writer, Producer & Director
Company: Purposed One Entertainment, LLC
Gift: Encouragement

A s a child and avid television viewer, Angela Johnson McGee learned about story, character, and structure by watching *Good Times, The Golden Girls,* and *The Cosby Show.* Her love for laughing and making others laugh provided her with a ticket to the entertainment capital of the world, Hollywood. And although her steps had been guided by God and she was now in Hollywood, her God-given purpose had not yet been revealed to her.

Lights!

She'd planned to work in the news industry, writing stories, and directing newscasts. That was her plan. But she soon discovered that God's plan is far greater and better than any plan we can create or envision. She learned that God had determined her destiny before she was born and it would be fulfilled.

"Three years after I graduated Eastern Illinois University, God not only positioned me closer to my destiny but he also provided the means for me to get there, that is, a job was waiting for me in an Los Angeles. Up until that point, my limited vision of television was what I had experienced in the newsroom. But when God anoints you, regardless of the feeling of uncertainty, you must move forward. To do anything less than going when God says go is to be disobedient. And that disobedience can cause you to miss out on the things He has planned for you.

"I was the youngest in my family. All of my siblings lived within one to 20 miles of my parents. I was a single mother of a 7 year-old daughter, and here I was embarking on a move that would take me more than 1,700 miles from my family to a place where I knew no one. Was this a faith walk? Oh yes it was."

Life is a journey of choices, and discernment demands that we choose, not between good and bad but between better and best. Discernment requires that we pray, study His word, seek Godly counsel from others about the possibilities, and then wait for God to reveal the next step. God's yearning, His will for us, will awaken our soul to the whisper of His Spirit.

"By not giving in to the fear of failing and the uncertainty of my future, I heeded God's call and journeyed to Hollywood. And because of that obedience, I became exposed to another level of entertainment. God had my steps ordered and life planned out. He connected me with the best in the business. I met with and was mentored by talented people like Yvette Lee Bowser, the creator of the sitcom *Living Single.* I learned a great deal from Yvette, and her mentoring paid off; I was accepted into the 'Marvin Hanks and Guy Miller Screenwriting Program,' which Bill and Camille Cosby established in the names of Camille's father and Bill's producer.

The Bible declares that your gifts will make room for you and put you before great men. And God's word is truth."

Camera!

Growing up, Angela was a self-proclaimed tomboy, playing basketball and softball, and most often against guys on the court or field. Looking back, she now knows that God was creating and developing her competitive nature through athletics, as she would need that same passion for victory to work God's plan for His Kingdom.

"God was grooming my gift of faith even in my youth and even before I knew I had faith. I think because of my willingness, commitment, and dedication to work hard as an athlete, God nurtured my mindset, shaping it so that I'd be one who never gives up. When faith is coupled with the attitude of a competitor, nothing is impossible. Someone recently complimented me on my stick-to-it-ness and said, 'I'm inspired by you because you never give up.' The thing is, I don't know how to give up. I don't know how to walk away. It's in my nature to keep pushing toward the mark —no matter what comes. Over the years, I've come to know that when God says He's going to do something, He will. If not now, then later. Our job is to persevere and be obedient to what He's called us to do. I've come to understand that God will not give a vision without giving provision. He is watching. The camera is rolling. And as the television or film director is at the helm of his or her productions, God, our director, is at the helm of the production of our lives. He sees the end before the beginning. He knows the outcome, and when we take His direction and follow His lead, we win in the end."

Action!

Angela's work in Hollywood eventually led her to the set of *Sister, Sister*, a sitcom about identical twin sisters, Tia and Tamera Landry, who were separated at birth and adopted by different families then reunited during a chance encounter while shopping at the mall. In the same way, we too are adopted into God's family and reunited with God when we align ourselves with his Son, Jesus, who welcomes us to Him as brothers and sisters.

"The cool thing about working on *Sister, Sister*," Angela says, "was that in real life the stars of the show, Tia and Tamera, were both born-again believers. Their mom, Mrs. Mowry, demanded a Christian set. There was no cussing on the set. There was no secular music played during rehearsal or the live taping, only gospel. The girls, their mom, and the entire cast prayed together before every show. And I believe because God was placed at the center of that set, the show was blessed for six successful seasons."

Roll It!

In addition to the gifts of faith and writing, Angela also credits God with her gift of encouragement.

"I really enjoy encouraging people. I think of talks I've had with individuals who were going through something and needed a little pick-me-up, and I recall how I lifted them up with words and prayers. I see myself with cheerleading pom-poms, reminding them who God is and how they shouldn't give up because God doesn't give up on us. I encourage people to never give up because the moment you do, you could be two seconds away from the thing God has in store for you, and if you quit, you'll never know it. So I say, believe and trust God, and know that no matter what happens, He's watching. The director is always watching.

"We are a chosen people. He chose us. He ordered our steps, ordained our lives, spoke our destinies, and anointed us with gifts for His purpose. It's His desire that we succeed, because our success is paramount to the success of furthering His Kingdom. And when we remember that our gifts are not merely for us, but for His Kingdom, our faith will continue to carry us by our belief that with Him, all things are possible."

Gift Wrap:

- When God anoints you, regardless of the feeling of uncertainty, you must move forward.

- Life is a journey of choices, and discernment demands that we choose, not between good and bad but between better and best.

- I encourage people to never give up because the moment you do, you could be two seconds away from the thing God has in store for you, and if you quit, you'll never know it. So I say, believe and trust God, and know that no matter what happens, He's watching. The director is always watching.

Angela's Other Gifts: Faith

CHAPTER 5

LOOK BEYOND THE DUMPS

Elayna Fernández: The Power of a Positive Purpose

> I will lift up mine eyes unto the hills, from whence
> cometh my help. My help cometh from the LORD.
> —PSALM 121

Name: Elayna Fernández
Position: Empowerment Teacher
and Marketing Strategist
Company: Designed 2 Impress
Spiritual Gifts: Faith

Elayna Fernández crawled through the trash at the dump. A tropical breeze rustled the banana trees, carrying the stench of human waste. In a few minutes the smell was not so bad. The flies, however, swarmed around her, landing on her legs and arms. A young boy approached and began gathering aluminum cans. He wore a pair of women's shoes that were too large for his feet. *Perhaps today I will find a treasure,* Elayna thought.

Lifting a soggy magazine, she tried to pronounce the name "icklits" she said out loud, looking at the "HIGHLIGHTS" magazine cover. Turning the front page, she looked at the happy children in the pictures—a young boy with yellow hair, a girl in a red skirt. Others kicked played baseball across a green field. The boy with the yellow hair wore white sneakers and a wide smile. Elayna thought it would be nice to live in a place such as this. Putting the magazine in her bag she hurried home.

Elayna visited the dump often to collect magazines. Before long, she had a small library in her tin-roof home. Looking at the pictures made her feel happy, gave her ideas. She made cardboard props, dreamed up stories and created characters based on the children she saw in her magazines. One day, when the power went out, she put on a puppet show. The kids in her neighborhood paid to attend. Elayna began to hold more performances. Soon she'd saved enough money to enroll in an English school. She spent long hours studying. For Elayna, though, the reading and "home work" wasn't work at all. It was a joy. In time, she began to tutor her classmates, earning more money.

Her entrepreneurship and ability to make and save money allowed her to save enough money to move to the big city. Going to college was not easy. Sometimes she had to walk many miles there and back, with no food on her stomach. She knew her goal, so she pressed on with faith and a positive attitude. Eventually, she would transfer from the public university to a private, nicer one, where she would excel just the same.

Just when she started to reap the benefits, Elayna faced something unexpected that would scar her and remove the characteristic smile on her face. She was the victim of an evil man's abduction. The tragedy affected her journey and she started to question her hardships. Six months after the horrible incident, she was victim of a car crash where no one had significant injuries but put her on an eight-day coma. Elayna could hear people around her say "Don't bother, she's done" and she felt glad. But then she also heard her family an best friends talk about the Elayna they knew and loved. Elayna detected the pattern to her life: survival, overcoming obstacles, and dealing with hardship was her way of life. She realized she had survived and she started to pursuit once again the life she'd seen in her "Highlights" magazine.

Elayna worked and studied harder than ever. Her proficiency in English and her excellent grades earned her an entry into the Work and Travel Program and a Visa to the United States. She worked hard that summer, traveled a lot and met a lot of people. Before she went back home, she also met the man who would become the father of her daughters and, eventually, the biggest challenge she'd ever face.

In 2001, Elayna left her successful career, family and friends and the first home she owned, and moved to California to start a family. Maybe her children would have the "Highlights" life she didn't have. With the birth of her daughters, Elayna's life seemed like a dream...but the pattern soon continued. Elayna was left a single mom of toddlers to start over again.

Elayna moved on. She used the same attitude that helped her survive and put faith on each of her actions. And moreover, she had a powerful, positive purpose: her children. Within 6 months, she bounced back from having no resources to working at a law firm and incorporating a business. Today, Elayna is a successful author, speaker and business woman, teaching others techniques on her happy life as a mother inspired her to create PositiveMommies.com.

"It's truly incredible how your attitude, how you view things can help you," Elayna says. "Even though I grew up poor as a child, I had a lot of joy, a lot of passion, a lot of motivation, and the ability to view, believe and work on my success. There are the five principles of success I teach others...."

See the Big Picture

"Vision is number one. You have to be able to see the big picture. Things may seem to go wrong or not going the way you want them to go but, if you have a vision of where you are headed, then the big picture parts will work themselves out."

Prepare For Blessings

"If you're ready for things to come your way and you prepare yourself to face a certain situation, then you'll act with confidence. One day, I said to my daughter, 'Oh no, it's raining outside.' But she says, 'It's okay, Mommy. We have an umbrella.' She was confident that it was going to be okay. And you know what? It was, because we had an umbrella. Kids are the best teachers! So, when we are prepared we can be confident things will turn out okay."

When you have stood in the middle of the furnace and survived, people pay attention to your words. Shadrack, Meshach and Abednego prayed, prepared and praised God *before* they walked into the flames. As a result, they turned disaster into victory, brought glory to God, and changed the culture of the land. Your actions will change the culture, too, when you prepare and listen to God's leading.

"I am very big on listening to God because, when you are on the right path and you're doing what He's called you to do, He will give you the guidance you need. I think that's one of my gifts, the ability to listen and be able to hear those inner promptings from God. For me, this gift of discernment is incredible. I've been presented with situations before where I've been blessed to know in advance the way I should go, and there is nothing that can compare to knowing that you're going the right direction before you arrive."

Be Diligent

"Another thing you need in order to be successful is diligence. You can't just wait for things to happen. It's okay to seek opportunities but sometimes you have to make them for yourself, too. You know, the person that works harder, the person that works smarter, is the person that's going to achieve success in the marketplace."

"It's not enough to just seek opportunities, we need to create our own and a lot of time we do that by networking, by meeting new people and getting to know what's beyond our own small world. You know, we are made in the image of the creator and because of that, we are called to create things. Some of the things we create are opportunities for ourselves."

Be Disciplined

"This is probably the hardest one for a lot of us—staying focused. If we make a habit of staying centered on the task, rather than becoming distracted with side issues, we definitely can reach our goal. I don't know anyone that has become successful that has not demonstrated a disciplined life. You don't need to be super organized or a neat freak, but you do need to remain focused on the prize. You need to know what steps are necessary to achieve your goal and the costs required. Don't start something you can't finish, but if you start it, don't stop til you do!"

Be Faithful

"Your faith is the piece that holds everything together" When you are faithful, you can see the big picture, you can be prepared, you can find the resilience and the strength to be diligent and you can find the will to be disciplined. So, I believe that first and foremost, faith is the energy that drives success. I am grateful for my faith in the Lord, for my faith in humankind, for my faith in myself and in my children. Faith truly moves mountains, because it helps us overcome every situation we face. If you don't think you can do it, if you're not sure the Lord is going to help you, then you won't achieve it. If you don't trust people, if you don't build relationships, if you don't believe that success can happen for you, then your lack of confidence and isolation will hold you back. God made us to connect with others, not to work alone. The body of Christ is all about networking with one another and, as a member of that body, we are called to encourage, uplift and counsel each other. That's faith—faith you can depend on—faith that will hold you when you hurt—faith that our lives matter to others even when we can't see the impact.

Faith is the key ingredient. If you're one of those people that doesn't like the world you live in, if you're always complaining and wishing the culture or circumstances were different, then teach your kids, have faith in your kids. Help them prepare for the future and contribute in a positive way so the world will become a better place. Teach them the beauty of life. Spend time with them. And tell them how much you love them. Be faithful in the small things, the raising of a child, and then you'll see that your life was a success. In fact, it was priceless."

Gift Wrap

- Things may seem to go wrong or not going the way you want them to go but, if you have a vision of where you are headed, then the big picture parts will work themselves out."

- You can't just wait for things to happen. It's okay to seek opportunities but sometimes you have to make them for yourself, too. You know, the person that works harder, the person that works smarter, is the person that's going to achieve success in the marketplace."

- We are made in the image of the creator and because of that, we are called to create things. Some of the things we create are opportunities for ourselves."

Elayna's Other Gift: Encouragement

CHAPTER 6

LET YOUR LIGHT SHINE

Pam Perry: It's Your Year, Decade and Life

"Carry each other's burdens, and in this way you will fulfill the law of Christ."

GALATIANS 6:2, NIV

Name: Pam Perry
Position: Partner
Company: Perry+Williamson
Spiritual Gifts: Helping

"Goooood morning, listeners, and welcome to another day of rain, ice, sleet, and snow, fender benders, ditch dodging, and guardrail ricochets as you sled to work. Not because you want to, not because it's smart to risk your life driving in these conditions, but because your boss will fire you if you don't. Meanwhile, your kids are home enjoying another snow day courtesy of your public education dollars. Listen for your credit card account to go *ka-ching* in a few minutes as a substantial transaction comes through to pay for the pizzas and soft drinks your child is ordering as a result of today's wintry fun. Speaking of fun, here's an oldie-but-goody to remind you that winter won't last forever, kids grow up too fast, and you should be home making snow cream, snow men, and memories instead of making a living at a job you hate. Hit it, Sly."

Through the plate glass window, Pam Perry watched as the disc jockey cued Sly & the Family Stone's "Hot Fun in the Summertime." Summertime. Fun. *What am I doing here, Pam wondered. Sure, I've got the cash, car, and career. Yes, I'm at the top of my game. But is this all there is? Was I really placed here on earth just to sell airtime and ads so listeners stuck in traffic could be harassed and cajoled into spending money on products and services they don't really need?* Walking away from the studio, she thought of her friend Andria Hall. Hall, a former CNN news anchor and national news correspondent for the FOX Network, had been at the top of her game, too. Then she was gone. Lost to breast cancer.

> If you want to achieve great success in business as a Christian, then you need to be very, very Christian, but also very, very business.
>
> —JOHN MAXWELL

The song ended and Pam stepped into the sales manager's office to review her account list. The easy listening music at the station was like so much of her life—familiar, comfortable, and old. Very, very old.

"When I thought of my friend Andria and the impact she'd had on those around her during her too-short life, something inside snapped. It was like a veil parted. Immediately, God took away my desire to sell ads. I mean, I'd been great at it. One of the best. But all of a sudden, I couldn't get any satisfaction from my work. It didn't make a difference to me how much money I made, how big my commission was. None of that mattered. I started spending a lot of time working with nonprofits and, without even realizing it, God placed a new calling in my heart. I found my joy came from serving others."

As Pam's nonprofit work began to develop, she found her true calling, her "God shape." And that profile took the shape of a servant. During her journey from "selling air" to serving others, Pam, as a development director for nonprofits, uncovered a passion for public relations, marketing, and acting.

"Pretty soon I got noticed for the work I was doing with nonprofits," she says. "One in particular was Joy of Jesus. When it became clear God had called me to a new work, I left the station and took a major pay cut. In my new job, I would work a hundred hours a week for what seemed like $100. But that was okay because I was full of joy. I was so excited about what I was doing. I'd look around and say, 'OK, you ready to roll? Let's roll! Come on. Let's get going!'"

Pam discovered what all great leaders learn: Passion produces results.

But Pam says that it's not enough to just have passion and vision. You have to be willing to work hard, persevere, and turn problems into stepping-stones.

"I hear people say all the time, 'This is going to be my year' or 'It's my decade,' and I think, *That's great. Good for you.* But if it's really going to be your year or your decade, you have to get your head in the game, light your lamp, and get to work. You can't be messing around with this Jesus business and think it's all going to just happen for you. You have to pray, prepare, and press forward. If your prayers don't have legs, then it's just wishful worship."

"The only way you're going to receive God's harvest is to get in the field and get serious about the work to which you've been called. For me, that's a bottom line precept from God. He called us to be stewards, to work, sow, and harvest. For my clients, that means rolling up the sleeves and getting busy about becoming successful.

"I meet a lot of people who want someone else to light their lamp, carry their torch, and shine the light on their good works, but Jesus is clear about this. We're to light our lamp and put it on a hill to guide others, not leave it under a basket to burn out. Too often that's what happens to a lot of people, though. They let their message grow moldy and die. Or, they're like the five foolish virgins, that is, they want someone else to do the work for them."

Invest in Others

"There's a group called The Anointed Authors on Tour. They travel to different parts of the country as a team, promoting their books and performing book signings. Each person has a set responsibility to make the tour a success. This is proof of how authors can gain great success by working together. Many authors have very similar topics. Their perspective may be a bit different, but both authors can benefit by creating buzz for their audiences and cut not only the cost but the work in half."

"Offer to blog about another author's new book, teaching topic, or business venture. Ask him or her to send bookmarks, flyers, and other freebies that you can give away from your site. Offer to host a virtual book signing table with autographed copies specifically for that site. Give, release, and watch God work."

"Linking back is the golden rule of Web marketing. Do unto others and they will, in turn, link back to you. You can also offer to link to various bookstores. Remember, when you add links to your site, you also increase traffic to your own site."

"Endorsements and word-of-mouth remain the most trusted forms of sales. Offer to include another author's content in your e-zine or newsletter, and ask if they would be willing to do the same for you. The better your content, the greater the chance someone will recognize you as an expert in your field. Offer to sell an author's book at your events. Ask them to do the same for you. Offer commission or an incentive to make it worth their time."

"Finally," Pam says, "no matter what you're doing, no matter where you are, you are a light, so be a positive witness for Christ, and let your walk glorify Him. That means in everything you do, strive for excellence."

Gift Wrap

- You can't be messing around with this Jesus business and think it's all going to just happen for you. You have to pray, prepare, and press forward. If your prayers don't have legs, then it's just wishful worship.

- "The only way you're going to receive God's harvest is to get in the field and get serious about the work to which you've been called. For me, that's a bottom line precept from God. He called us to be stewards, to work, sow, and harvest. For my clients, that means rolling up the sleeves and getting busy about becoming successful.

- No matter what you're doing, no matter where you are, you are a light, so be a positive witness for Christ, and let your walk glorify Him. That means in everything you do, strive for excellence.

Pam's Other Gift: Teaching

CHAPTER 7

GIFTED TO SERVE OTHERS

Derrick L. Miles: Encouraging People to Achieve Superhuman Performance

After the reading from the Law and the Prophets, the synagogue rulers sent word to them, saying, "Brothers, if you have a message of encouragement for the people, please speak."

—ACTS 13:15, NIV

> **Name:** Derrick L. Miles
> **Position:** Chairman & CEO
> **Company:** The Milestone Brand
> **Gift:** Encouragement

Hope deferred makes the heart sick, but a dream fulfilled is a tree of life.

—PROVERBS 13:12, NIV

Derrick L. Miles lived a balanced life; he carried a chip on both shoulders. Young and black with a dual master's degree from one of the top programs in Health Administration,

Derrick attacked the corporate world confident he'd find a successful career as a health care executive. But on his climb up the ladder of success, Derrick found not just riches and success but dissatisfaction, fatigue, and frustration.

"Every new promotion ended the same way," says Derrick. "I'd nail the interview, land the job, and begin bubbling over with excitement. Then about three months into the job, the honeymoon would wear off, and I'd catch a whiff of the toxic environment that percolated in the cubicles and offices around me. After a few runs at this, I began to see the lethargic atmosphere for what it was: burnout. The people around me lacked fulfillment. Worse, their malaise was contagious. Soon, I became ineffective and discouraged. No matter how significant my contributions were in the areas of increased revenue, efficiencies, and cost avoidance, I found myself going from being eager to egging myself on. *Come on, Derrick, you can do better.*"

In 2002, Gallop conducted a study of engagement in the marketplace and found that only 28 percent of workers were considered engaged in their work. Gallop defined these individuals as motivated, energized and eager to use their gifts, talents, and training in their everyday work. "We call these people Superhuman Performers," Derrick says.

The largest segment of the workforce (54 percent) collect a paycheck but do little to advance the mission of the company for which they work. "Basically, they're asleep at the wheel," says Derrick. "Sure, they contribute, but there's no passion or energy in their effort."

The smallest segment of workers, but still a substantial number (17 percent), are actually working against the company. They don't like their job and want others to know it, including the company's customers. Gallop estimates that this subset alone costs U.S. corporations $350 billion each year in loss productivity.

"The first time I saw that figure I was shocked," says Derrick, "but the longer I remained in the corporate culture, the more I came to see the statistics were dead on. As a former executive, I saw firsthand how stark the difference was between the 28 percent that's engaged, motivated, and moving forward and the rest who are just taking up space and pulling down a paycheck. The old adage proved true again: 20 percent of the people were doing 80 percent of the work. Once I saw the great need for people to become engaged in their calling, I knew I had to act. That's why I helped start Milestone Motivation. I wanted to help others find not just work but fulfillment in their work.

Stage Fright

Dreams tormented Derrick. Not scary dreams like nightmares but dreams of success.

"When I was around 24 years old I began to dream about speaking in front of large audiences with a message of how I could help others achieve peak performance. I'd wake up in the morning pumped and start my day off full of energy. But deep down, I think, I never really believed that dream would ever come. You see, going back to my years as a teen I'd always been terrified of speaking. It wasn't just a little stage fright. I would shake 'til I'd sweat —then shake some more. I like to say I had a lot of nervous energy, and I did, but that power caused me to grasp the sides of the podium and hold on so tight it would begin to vibrate. If one leg or side was shorter than the other I'd know because of how hard I'd rock that pedestal. My hands shook, my legs buckled. Even my eyelids quivered.

"Then one evening something told me, *Study the top decile communicators.* And that's just what I did. I observed the best speakers, people like Zig Ziglar, Leslie Calvin Brown, and Keith Harrell. I read books, and I practiced —a lot.

"Through research I found out that some of the people I admired like TD Jakes and Peter Daniels also struggled with extreme nervousness when speaking in public. Through practice I became so good that when I was introduced as the executive speaker for my last corporation, the person introducing me announced, 'You are in for a treat this morning because Derrick Miles will speak to you today on…,' and I knew I'd reached my goal. At that moment I didn't feel fear; I felt like a superhuman!

"Later that same evening, the whisper I heard before said, *It's time, Derrick. Time for you to speak to the universe and share your message of motivation with others. They need to hear what you know. You need to help them become equipped and use their gifts to experience Superhuman Performance.* I'm not the only one who's heard this small voice. Others can attest to its authority. And I'm firmly convinced that if you've heard a similar calling then it's time for you to claim your destiny and begin living in the realm of Superhuman Performance."

Superhuman Performance

In the current economy, where massive layoffs are epidemic, increased productivity is the mantra of management, *semi-permanent unemployment* is an accepted euphemism for *retirement,* and your ability to outperform and outproduce are the keys to job stability. "I believe we all benefit when performance improves," says Derrick. "We sell more services, produce exceptional products, and develop better leaders. Let's face it. We're all judged on our performance. I don't care if you're a ball team, coach, or kindergarten teacher. Your performance will determine how far you go. We're even judged in our homes. My wife is constantly evaluating my performance as being a husband and father—and she doesn't grade on a curve."

Laid Off & Let Loose

> A gift opens the way and ushers the giver into the presence of the great.
>
> —PROVERBS 18:16, NIV

Derrick was judged by his performance and deemed valuable to the corporation. But in the new global economy even the most valuable employee is expendable. When the word trickled down that there would be layoffs, Derrick didn't panic. In fact, he felt a sense of freedom, as if he was about to be kicked from the nest and ordered to fly.

"Several months prior to the layoff I was feeling the urge to do something different. Once again, I'd reached the point in my job where I lacked fulfillment. My desire to encourage others, uplift, and inspire far outweighed any mandate to cut costs or develop a new service line. I saw my fellow workers struggling to make sense of what was happening in the marketplace, on Wall Street, and on Main Street. I read their body language, and it wasn't good. So many had slipped into the realm of active disengagement. They seemed to be living a life they absolutely hated just to pay mortgages, light bills, and taxes.

"The announcement came down that a 'resource action' was imminent. I had a decision to make. I could take another job and begin a new cycle of honeymoon, fulfillment, flat line production, and frustration ending in fatigue, or I could embrace my gifts and do the thing I felt called to do.

"I chose to jump from the nest. My decision was aided, in part, by my former organization who provided a handsome severance package that opened the way for me to speak and coach people free of charge. I began to notice that the demand for my message gained in popularity. We'd hit a sweet spot in the corporate culture. With the help of my brother, Darrayl, we formed The Milestone Brand and launched a radio program called Milestone Motivation. Because of the show's success, it has since grown into what is now The Superhuman Performance Radio Broadcast."

The Superhuman Performance Radio Broadcast

The Superhuman Performance Radio Broadcast allows executives, entrepreneurs, celebrities, and faith-based leaders to express how their gifts and passions have helped them exceed their own expectations and make a difference in the marketplace. "It wasn't long before people from all over the world began to call," says Derrick. "I was contacted by people in Australia, Ukraine, Romania, Macedonia, Nigeria, and Germany, to name a few. All wanted to be a part of The Superhuman Performance Radio Broadcast, and the stories resonated with our listeners. So much so that we were advised to create a book to help others understand how using their gifts can lead to powerful life changes, not just in the individual but in the larger community.

"The concept of a book, however, took me out of my comfort zone. I'd learned business writing in graduate school, but I had no clue how to write and organize a nonfiction book, especially one that would captured the soul of the individual stories of our guests. But a friend of mine, Cam Marston, suggested that I find someone gifted in writing to help us shape the book. I interviewed several writers, but it was my brother's gift of discernment that led us to Eddie Jones. A few weeks later, we were reintroduced to Ricc Rollins, a publicist and former talk show host. Ricc pitched our book idea to a national television firm, and they agreed to market our project nationwide.

"Fast forward a few more weeks, and I'm talking with Keith Harrell who agrees to serve as my coach. He recommended we split the project into two books with each one featuring seven gifts. While it seems that all of these pieces fell into place in a very short period of time, I sincerely believe the process began much earlier, perhaps in my early twenties. That's because even back then I felt as if I was being prepared to encourage others to use their gifts to achieve Superhuman Performance."

Don't Rob the Universe

We began this book with the story of Walt Disney and how his vision for Disneyland changed the landscape of not just entertainment but the industry of imagination. Picture Orlando without Walt Disney World, southern California without Disneyland, and animated movies without *Toy Story*. Had Walt Disney agreed with his friend Arthur Linkletter that a dusty field with orange groves would always be just a vast wasteland of wishful wonderings, then we would have been robbed of laughter and the vision of a world of imagination. Derrick recalls the story of John Lasseter, Chief Creative Officer at Pixar.

"Lasseter was working as an animator at Walt Disney Feature Animation," Derrick explains, "but felt something was missing. After the movie *101 Dalmatians*, the studio began to repeat itself, relying on stale ideas that proved predictably profitable and boring."

After his sudden departure from Disney, John teamed up with Alvy Ray Smith and Ed Catmull at Lucasfilm and produced the first computer animated short *The Adventures of André* and Wally B. John's original idea had been to create only the backgrounds on computers, but in the final version, everything was generated by computer, including the characters. Lucasfilm was eventually acquired by Steve Jobs and became Pixar. From 1986 onward, John oversaw all of Pixar's films, personally directing *Toy Story, A Bug's Life, Toy Story 2,* and *Cars*. John has won two Academy Awards and has been nominated numerous times. His short film *Knick Knack* was selected by original Monty Python member Terry Gilliam as one of the ten best animated films of all time.

"Imagine how we would have been robbed if John Lasseter hadn't pursued his dreams," says Derrick. "Suppose he had believed those who had told him 'It's not possible.' I'm firmly convinced your dreams are a clear indication of your ultimate purpose on earth. When you make a commitment to utilize your gifts, people arrive (almost magically) to assist you and encourage you to push forward with the desires in your heart.

"By reading the stories in this book, you are already steps ahead of where I was when I began my journey. I didn't have a roadmap or a mentor that helped me utilize those gifts that I had inside of me. I actually realized my gifts through trial and error —and a lot of it. To help you discover your area of giftedness, we have created the Milestone Marketplace Gift Assessment. I would encourage you to use it. Don't rob the universe of the gifts given to you. Share with them with others, plumb the depths of your imagination. Reach for planets not yet seen. Your greatness isn't your education, experience, or economic contribution to society. It's the gift inside you waiting to burst forth."

Gift Wrap

- Find fulfillment in your work to alleviate burnout, frustration, and ineffectiveness, and in your work, use your gifts.

- It's time for you to claim your destiny and begin living in the realm of Superhuman Performance.

- When you make a commitment to utilize your gifts, people arrive (almost magically) to assist you and encourage you to push forward with the desires in your heart.

Derrick's Other Gifts: Administration

CHAPTER 8

MONEY WON'T MAKE YOU RICH, OBEDIENCE TO GOD'S CALLING WILL

Pastor Sunday Adelaja: Abundance Through Stewardship

> And the LORD said, "I will cause all my goodness to pass in front of you, and I will proclaim my name, the LORD, in your presence. I will have mercy on whom I will have mercy, and I will have compassion on whom I will have compassion.
> —EXODUS 33:19, NIV

Name: Pastor Sunday Adelaja
Position: Founder and Senior Pastor
Company: Embassy of God
Gift: Compassion

Sunday Sunkanmi Adelaja approached the front door of the State University in Belarus, eager to begin his studies. Far from Nigeria, his home, Sunday sought a warm apartment and friends, but finding fellowship and a church in which to worship proved difficult among the cold, dark streets in Minsk. In the months and weeks that followed, Sunday began to sense a growing silence from God and a deepening solitude that prompted him to lock himself in his apartment. "I will stay in this room until you appear," he whispered to God. "I will remain until I get a confirmation that you are with me."

For days, Sunday prayed, refusing to leave his room. He would pray five, ten, fifteen hours some days. On the fifth, God appeared to him in dreams. God began to speak, not in a general way but with specific instructions of what he must do next. "God called me," Sunday would say later. "He became real and personal."

Sunday knew what he must do next. He would start a church among a people who believed there was no God. He would bring hope and a future to a culture that had known only darkness and despair. "They will fight you," he heard God say. "They will resist you. But you will prevail. You will have power and strength in my name."

An Army of One

> The first purpose of employment should be to bring
> God's kingdom to rule in our workplace.
> —PASTOR SUNDAY ADELAJA

"When I came to Russia, it was really very scary," Pastor Sunday explains. "There was no church, no pastors, and few Christians. I tried to find God at work, but it was hard, especially for a black man. The people of Belarus called me 'nigger,' 'monkey,' and 'chocolate.' So today when I hear African Americans complaining about racism, I want to laugh. They have no idea what racism really is. If you want to see bigotry, you need to come to Russia."

At nights, Pastor Sunday would invite others into his home, showing them his picture of Jesus and sharing Scripture with them. The authorities threatened to have him arrested. Pastor Sunday persisted. His small flock grew. But he could not escape the social stigma of his roots. His dark skin led to taunts and racial slurs, so after graduation he tried to return to Nigeria, but his departure was denied due to his missionary activities. Pastor Sunday settled in Kiev. He would stay and work where God had planted him.

"It seemed almost impossible that God would call me to start a church in Russia. *Who would come to hear a black man preach?* Why would someone who called me "monkey" come to church to hear what I had to say? For four years I tried to start a church but not one European would come. Others came. People from Asia and Africa. But no Russians.

"Then I heard God say, 'Go look for the down-and-out people, for those who are broken. Go to the outcasts. Search for the alcoholics, drug addicts. Just go love them. Don't preach to them. Don't try to pull them to church. Just love on them.'

"I went like Jesus and visited people in prison. I fed the hungry, clothed the naked. And through my obedience, God did a wonderful thing. We began having alcoholics and drug addicts come to our church in mass. In one year, our church went from 0 to 1,000 members. Today, our church is the only one in the world where the membership is 99.8 percent white and the pastor is black. I'm almost the only black among whites."

Money Won't Make You Rich

In the United States, however, Pastor Sunday sees a completely different landscape, one divided not by skin color but by income.

"In America, I see a society that worships deliberately and the god of money is the mountain everyone wants to climb. If you reach the summit, everybody is supposed to worship you—even if you have the wrong values. People who are financially successful are revered. It doesn't matter what kind of value system they have. The morals of the rich may be horrible, but they're worshiped. They're on the cover of magazines and on TV shows. Everybody wants to see them and be like them.

"This mindset has even infiltrated the church, especially the mega-churches where money is a big thing. Not all large churches are like this, of course. But I see a lot who put a large emphasis on wealth. It's become the way they measure the value of their members. You are accepted into a congregation based on how successful are you, how much you earn, and what your achievements are.

"But with God, making money is not a big deal. It's just a matter of choice. That's why I wrote my book *Money Won't Make You Rich*. I wanted to prove to people that becoming a millionaire is not a big deal, that making money and becoming successful by the world's standards is not a big deal. Being able to live right with money, however —that is where the challenge is."

Rich in Stewardship

"The whole reason we have money is for stewardship," Pastor Sunday says. "If you have money and you cannot serve the less privileged and the unfortunate, then you are poor. Money won't make you rich. Only your heart can make you rich. You've got to be rich in values, virtues, and character. You have to be rich in the things that matter to God. Having money is not a measure of success, but stewardship is.

"To my fellow brothers who believe in the prosperity gospel, I say, 'Preach about prosperity in the right way. Don't just preach prosperity, telling people that they only need to bring money to the church, to put it in the hands of the pastor.' I've seen a lot of pastors in America who have a lot of money because they take up big offerings, and yet their people remain broke. When you preach that the way to get prosperity is to bring offering and tithes to the church but leave members of your congregation desperate and poor, then you are not acting as a good steward. Too often the only person benefiting from the prosperity gospel is the preacher.

"God taught Adam how to be prosperous, and I believe that principle still applies today. God put Adam in the Garden of Eden and told him to work. He told him to till the ground and make it productive. We need to teach people the laws of money. We need to teach people the principles of savings and the culture of thrift. We need to teach people to be diligent and faithful in developing their skills. A lot of those churches don't teach people these things. They don't take time to train people how to do things God's way. They just tell them to bring the money to the church and pray that God will bless them, but the only way you can really make wealth is to work for it. People need to understand the laws of money. I want people to know that money is not a big deal. What is a big deal is the values you have with how you use your money. Money is a responsibility. It is a trust from God and an obligation to stewardship."

Rich in Spiritual Work

For Pastor Sunday, being rich in the things of God is the essence of true wealth, and for him, that begins with a devoted prayer life.

"You can use these gifts in the marketplace, in the supermarket, or in a public park," Pastor Sunday says. But when it comes to the marketplace, you have to be very strategic. When I meet people for business, I want to listen to what God is telling me about them. Often I'll ask questions during a business meeting to draw out what's on their heart. After the meeting, I might say, 'I don't mean to pry, but I'm a believer, and I feel like I should pray for your family.' I might sense that their wife has cancer or some other disease. I might see a challenge with their children. Whatever it is, if we're sensitive to the leading of God's Spirit, we will know how to pray for people, and in doing so, we are dispensing God's blessings —and His riches. Money won't make you rich. However, obedience to God's calling will in more ways than you can imagine."

Gift Wrap

- Becoming a millionaire is not a big deal. Making money and becoming successful by the world's standards is not a big deal. Being able to live right with money, however—that is where the challenge is.

- God put Adam in the Garden of Eden and told him to work. He told him to till the ground and make it productive. We need to teach people the laws of money. We need to teach people the principles of savings and the culture of thrift. We need to teach people to be diligent and faithful in developing their skills.

- Money won't make you rich. However, obedience to God's calling will in more ways than you can imagine."

Sunday's Other Gifts: Teaching

CHAPTER 9

HOW TO DISCOVER & PRACTICE YOUR SPIRITUAL GIFTS

Elmer Towns: Let Liberty Reign

Teach them his decrees and instructions, and show
them the way they are to live and how they are to
behave.

—EXODUS 18:20, NIV

Name: Elmer Towns
Position: Co-Founder and Dean
Company: Liberty University
Spiritual Gifts: Teaching

Elmer Towns peddled his bike down a street shaded by
large oaks bearded with Spanish moss and passed a stand
of palmetto trees guarding the banks of a creek. Elmer caught
the odor of low-tide mud banks basking under the heat of the
summer sun and saw brown-skinned boys wading hip deep

into the marsh as they herded blue crabs into a burlap sack. Turning the corner, he slowed long enough to fling a newspaper onto the front porch of a two-story house. Then, pumping the pedals, he raced home, his tires rumbling over the wooden planks as he sped away from private gardens and the lattice archways of Savannah's upper class.

That evening, alone in his room with a ringed notebook in his lap escaped to the Mississippi River, creating a tale of German sailors, stealth submarines, and the mischievous antics of two grandmothers. The WWII story lacked a compelling plot, character depth, and dramatic dialogue, but Elmer didn't notice, nor would it have mattered. The novel, a homework assignment, was his creation, and he filled his entire writing tablet. Without knowing it, his fifth grade teacher had helped launch the career of a new writer.

"Elmer, in all my years of teaching, I've never seen a report as thorough and well-written as this one. I learned more from your report on the Panama Canal than any I've ever read. I want you to do something for me. I want you to read as much as you can and as often as you can. I want you to read newspapers and books. Be disciplined about your use of time, and write constantly."

Later that year submitted "The History of the Wars Between China and Japan," a 99-page term paper. The completion of the project taught young Elmer two things: One, he could research, and two, he could write long documents in stunning detail.

"I enrolled in Columbia Bible College in South Carolina," Dr. Towns says. "That's where I met my wife, Ruth. My time at Columbia Bible College was a turning point. It helped me develop a deeper Christian life and a mastery of the English Bible. During my junior year, I commuted to Savannah where I opened and pastored Westminster Presbyterian, a church that had been closed for some time. The summer between my junior and senior years, though, I transferred to Northwestern College. It was there that I was introduced to northern evangelism, which was different from my southern revival roots."

"When I was young and just starting out in the ministry, I tried to do everything. I remember once holding an evangelistic service where I preached for a solid week, trying to get people saved. I can still remember the agony of standing there, making that altar call and watching to see if anyone would come forward. But nobody came and nobody got saved. Next, I tried to be a music leader. I took trombone lessons. Nothing. I tried everything, but I just wasn't seeing any fruit. Then, toward the end of my senior year at Northwestern, I gave a report in class. Afterwards, the professor asked me to stop by his office. He said, 'Elmer, that was an excellent report. Have you ever thought about being a Bible college teacher?'

"Now what he didn't know was that I'd always wanted to teach but thought you had to have 20 years of experience and be old. He looked at me and said, 'You don't teach your experience. You teach the Word of God. Experience only illustrates what you're teaching.'"

"The day before I was to start the fall semester of my final year at Dallas Seminary, I got a call asking if I'd teach a missions class at Dallas Bible College. The professor had just been called back to the mission field. I've always said, when God gives you an open door, walk through it. So, I began teaching even before I received my divinity degree, and I've been teaching in Bible colleges ever since."

In 1971, Jerry Falwell, Senior Pastor of Thomas Road Baptist Church in Lynchburg, Virginia, called Elmer and asked him to help start a Bible college. Together, the pair co-founded Lynchburg Baptist College that eventually became Liberty University. "Looking back," Elmer says, "I can see how God was preparing me for this new journey. I'd been President of Winnipeg Bible College for five years and had taught at Trinity Evangelical Divinity School, so my expertise as a college administrator proved invaluable as Jerry and I began to capture the vision of what God planned for this new college. We began with 154 students housed in small homes around Thomas Road Baptist Church. Today, I'm Dean of the School of Religion and Vice President of a university with a total student enrollment of over 73,000 (12,760 residential and 61,000 online)."

"Around 1992 or '93, Jerry asked me to write a spiritual gift inventory. He said, 'I've got about 50,000 people I want to give this to.' I could do that with no problem, I told him. Then he said, 'And, I need it Monday morning.' I thought he was kidding. There was no way I could turn around a project like that on such short notice. But Jerry wouldn't budge. He said, 'I know you've already been working with this. You can do it.'

"That weekend we got 26 inches of snow, and I was stuck at my desk. I couldn't get out. Sunday morning I was able to find a man who came by in a four-wheel-drive vehicle and drove me to church so I could teach Sunday school, but then all Sunday afternoon and the rest of Monday and Tuesday and into Wednesday morning, I did nothing but work on Jerry's spiritual gift inventory. This Spiritual Gift Inventory is available free on elmertowns.com."

In 2001 and his wife, Ruth, released, *Women Gifted For Ministry: How To Discover And Practice Your Spiritual Gifts.* Many of the principles discussed in their book were discovered during that prolonged weekend in '93. For anyone seeking to discern his or her spiritual gift Elmer offers the following advice.

"First, pay attention to the desires placed within you. For many people, the initial indication that God is calling them to a particular work manifests itself as an inner desire, a longing to serve or help others for a specific project. In the beginning, this nudging may feel like a burden placed upon your heart. Think of this heaviness as God's Spirit, His mantle of favor, coming to rest upon you. Once you agree to His leading and move in obedience, you will experience a sense of joy. Second, seek to serve others on a frequent basis through your unique abilities. When you do, you will begin to identify your spiritual gifts, and you will find satisfaction and fulfillment in doing them. Third, remember that when you work within your area of gifting, you will find yourself both spent and renewed on a regular basis. This pouring out and drawing in parallels the life of Jesus who freely gave to all who asked and freely received from His Father."

One is joy. You experience that when you find your gift and use it for the benefit of others. Two, you're more profitable. Three, you're more spiritual because you're in tune with the Holy Spirit.

Gift Wrap

- Understanding your natural abilities may help you discover and develop your spiritual gifts, but God often uses people with limited or no ability to do great works. So, don't assume *you* are the only one God can use for a specific task. In some cases, He will use less qualified individual for a particular work in order to demonstrate His glory through their weakness.

- Someone who has the gift of faith ought to be at the very top of a company because executives are people with vision. They inspire, lead, and motivate, and that takes faith, faith in your people and faith that your decisions are correct.

- There are three benefits to using your gifts in the business setting. One is joy. You experience that when you find your gift and use it for the benefit of others. Two, you're more profitable. Three, you're more spiritual because you're in tune with the Holy Spirit.

Elmer's Other Gifts: Administration & Writing

CHAPTER 10

ONE PLUS ONE EQUALS 11, NOT TWO

George Fraser: Building Extraordinary Relationships

And he has filled him with the Spirit of God, with
wisdom, with understanding, with knowledge and
with all kinds of skills

—EXODUS 35:31, NIV

> **Name:** George C. Fraser
> **Position:** Chairman & CEO
> **Company:** FraserNet, Inc.
> **Gift:** Wisdom

Putnam Avenue, Brooklyn, New York, circa 1945.

You need three networks: personal (home);
operational (work) and strategic (community).

—GEORGE C. FRASER

A Guyanese immigrant hurries across the tracks of a rail-
road freight yard boxed in by boarded-up businesses. The

snapping and snarling of a yard dog guarding a car dealership spurs the man along, hands shoved into his pockets, collar pulled up. Snow erases his tracks as he moves into the darkness of a train trestle. An east wind brings the acrid odor of the coal-burning stoves and campfires of the homeless. Nearby, a gang of youths gathers in the shadows, passing out stolen goods from a boxcar. Ahead at the corner, under the halo of a street lamp, a policeman walks his beat. Far away, the Guyanese man hears the wail of an infant and his heart sinks. *Too many,* he thinks. *Already too many to feed. The boys, they must go. Girls, too. I will do this thing. For them and me. It is their only hope.*

"I was born into a family of 11 children," George C. Fraser says. "Eight boys and three girls. My father came to America from Guyana and married Ida Mae Baldwin, a woman from Lumpkin, Georgia. When I turned three, my mother became mentally ill and was institutionalized. My dad was a cab driver and worked 12- to 14-hour days. So when I was three, he put me in an orphanage. Brothers and sisters, too. But when I was five, because there were too many of us for one family, they busted us up, putting us in foster homes. And that's where I stayed until I turned 17."

"When I turned 17, I aged out of the foster care program," George explains. "What I mean by that is, I became a liability. In the State of New York, parents aren't paid to care for a child who's 17, so I had to find another place to live. I went back home to the brownstone that my father maintained in Brooklyn. When I got there, though, I found my brothers had aged out, too, and were hooked on heroin. I could either live in my dad's house with heroin dealers and addicts or move out.

"While in New York, I graduated from high school with a vocational diploma in woodworking. Guidance counselors kept telling me to drop out, that I wasn't college material. But I knew an education was the key to getting out of there. To pay my way through college, I mopped floors on the midnight shift at LaGuardia Airport."

"As soon as I could, I packed what little I had and took a Greyhound bus to Cleveland, Ohio. I didn't even tell my family where I was for a long time. Wanted to make sure I had my act together first."

"God has put each of us here with a unique purpose in mind," George says. "There's a job that He's assigned only you to do. And if you do not do it, the task will not get done. So, the world depends on every person to discover his or her purpose, to go down that path and to go through the pain of figuring out what that is. And by pain, I mean suffering through the mistakes, the failing. You must first be willing to branch out, to do something badly before you will ever be able to do it well. Life is a journey, and this journey is a quest to find out what the Creator put us here to do. Every pebble, every stone, every blockade, every fence put in our way has a purpose. Every trial is preparing us for the work that we're to do."

"I've been asked if I would change anything in my life, and the answer is: absolutely not. Because every trial and every tribulation serves to prepare you for a greater good, the real question is what did you learn from your experience that you could share with others that would help them? And for me, the answer: Successful people have the ability to remove toxic people and bloodsuckers from their lives.

> Very good will get you fired. Today, you've got to be amazing.
>
> —GEORGE C. FRASER

"It's the lesson I learned and one I've observed countless times in the lives of others. I've met literally thousands of successful people, and they all have this unique ability to extract themselves from people who drain their time, energy, and patience. Now, this is very easy to say but extraordinarily difficult to do because most of these people are your family. They're your significant others. Most of these people are your so-called friends. So there is tremendous psychological and social pressure on you to keep these people in your life.

> Education is just the "table stakes" to get you into the game. Your opportunities for success depend upon your ability to build relationships
>
> —GEORGE C. FRASER

"There's an old saying that goes, 'If you love something, set it free. If it comes back, it will always be yours. But, if it doesn't come back, it was never yours to begin with.' Well, there's a big *but* on that. If the thing you're trying to set free sits in your living room, messes up all your stuff, eats all your food, uses your cell phone, takes your money, and doesn't appear to realize that you've set it free, you either married it or gave birth to it. That's why removing these toxins from your life is so difficult to do. But I will tell you, again: If you're not able to do this, you will fail. Period.

"How do I know? Because I had to do it myself. How do I know? Because President Obama had to do this exact same thing in view of the American public. He had to deliver himself from his pastor of 20 years, a man who'd married him and his wife and who'd christened his two children. He didn't want to do it, but the relationship had turned toxic. And if he had not done this, we would not be calling him President Obama today. This is an important and powerful lesson that few people talk about because it's so sensitive. But everyone needs to know it because it's a key to success. Let me say it differently. Introduce me to your five closest friends, and that will tell me who you are."

"Don't spend major time with minor people," George says. "People who are going nowhere want you to go nowhere with them. People doing nothing want you to do nothing with them. If you want to change your life, change your relationships. If you are a 10 but you're hanging out with fives, pretty soon you'll be a five. The other piece of advice is don't hang out with broke people because if you hang out with broke people, pretty soon you're gonna be broke. Your relationships are everything. Your ability to build those relationships and to surround yourself with powerful and positive people that want at least as much as you want, if not more, is everything."

"I don't care how much education you have," George says. "By itself it's not enough to make you succeed. I've met people, very smart people who can't do very much. In fact, there are a lot of people who are educated derelicts. They have not converted their education into marketable skills. They've got all kinds of degrees, but they're still broke. So on the three-legged stool of life, the first leg on the stool is education. Get as much education as you can afford or stand. Then, understand that life is about lifelong learning, that you never stop learning, that education provides you the ticket to get into the ballpark of life so that you can play in the game. But then once you go into the ballpark, what are you going to see? Eighty thousand other people in that ballpark, and many, if not most of them, have more or better education than you.

"I've been in business for 23 years. I've worked for Procter & Gamble, United Way, and Ford Motor Company, and the mantra I heard growing up was, 'Get a good education, get a good job.' But that's not the mantra that I taught my two children. I told them to get a good education and create a job —for themselves and for their children. So while education is the first leg of the stool and profoundly important, it's not enough."

"The final leg on the stool of life is relationships, that is, your ability to work with and through other people; your ability to cultivate, nurture, and develop relationships at work, at home, and in the community; your ability to lead and to know when to follow; and your ability to love and to like people and to have people love and like you. None of this is about simply connecting, it's all about following up. I know people that have modest education, decent marketable skills, but the personality of a box of rocks. These people can't get along at work with anybody, and usually they're on the lowest rung of the ladder. If you graduated from Harvard, Yale, Morehouse, or Spellman but can't relate to people, you're book-smart but limiting your success in the marketplace.

"I also know people with a very modest education, strong marketable skills, and superior people skills. Their ability to cultivate, nurture, and develop relationships at work, at home, and in the community is superior. Their ability to love and to like people is superior. Their ability to lead and to know when to follow is superior. And these people are at the highest rung of every ladder in every organization, and these are the people that you will ultimately work for. These are the people leading everything. The smartest people aren't the leaders. The people who lead are the ones with superior interpersonal and people skills. I'm not pooh-poohing education. I'm just saying, it's not everything. What is everything are your relationships. That will determine how far you go in life."

> The winners in the competitive selling arena of our difficult economy are those who are the low-risk providers, not the low-price people.
>
> —DAVE KAHLE

George offers these additional truths for building extraordinary relationships:

- Give first, share always, and rewards will come later.

- It's important to think, feel, and believe that you are awesome.

- Superior interpersonal skills trump all other skills.

- What are you not doing because you're scared? Amazing people transcend their normal tasks and become leaders.

- Most business decisions are made at an emotional level then are justified by facts.

- Be nice to people. They will forget what you did, forget what you said, but they will not forget how you made them feel.

- The words you speak today are waiting for you tomorrow.

- The ultimate goal of all networking is to click, to make one plus one equal 11, not two. You click when chemistry, fit, and timing are in perfect alignment.

Gift Wrap:

- Find out what the marketplace needs and wants and is willing to pay for, and then develop your skills to fill that gap.

- "The final leg on the stool of life is relationships, that is, your ability to work with and through other people; your ability to cultivate, nurture, and develop relationships at work, at home, and in the community; your ability to lead and to know when to follow; and your ability to love and to like people and to have people love and like you.

- Successful people all have this unique ability to extract themselves from people who drain their time, energy, and patience.

George's Other Gift: Leadership

CHAPTER 11

PREPARATION, POSTURE, POSITION

Dr. Mark J. Chironna: The Three Ps to Superhuman Performance

He will show you a large room upstairs, furnished and ready. Make *preparation*s for us there."

MARK 14:15, NIV

Name: Dr. Mark J. Chironna
Position: Founder and Senior Pastor
Company: The Master's Touch
International Church
Gift: Teaching

The Jordan River ran at flood stage, overflowing its banks as snowmelt from Mount Hermon rushed through Caesarea Philippi, into the Hula Valley, and over the reeds and cattails that marked the headwaters of Lake Gennesaret. To the east lay sand storms and desert raiders. To the south, the Sea of Salt,

Desert of Sin, and the graves of those who'd doubted God's deliverance into the Promised Land. Now, the children of Egyptian slaves, God's chosen people, camped along the banks of the swollen river, their path blocked. Adam's ford, now submerged under flood waters, threatened to sweep away any who dared to cross. Once again, God had led His people to the edge of disaster. Gone, too, was their great leader, Moses.

In his place was a new prophet, experienced but untested. Joshua stood beneath the shade of a eucalyptus tree and saw the goodness of God across the river: clusters of grapes so full of juice that two men would be needed to carry them; pomegranates as big as a man's fist; hives of honey; and herds of sheep. He also saw the marl plateaus that marked the eastern edge of the Judaean desert, the distant city of Jericho, and the swirling tendrils of dust eddies as the approaching armies gathered to defend their land from the hordes of Hebrew men and women. Yes, the land that lay before him was good and pleasing, truly a land of promise. But taking the land would not be easy. It would exact a price and demand preparation, a posture of submission and careful positioning.

This journey from slavery to freedom would also require great faith. For three days, the officers had gone through the camp, giving orders to the people, preparing them to advance. "When you see the Ark of the Covenant of the LORD your God, and the Levitical priests carrying it, you are to move out from your positions and follow it. Then you will know which way to go, since you have never been this way before." (Joshua 3:3-4, NIV) "Consecrate yourselves," Joshua had told the people yesterday, "for tomorrow the Lord will do amazing things among you....Call the priests together. Take up the Ark of the Covenant, and pass on ahead of the people."

Trumpets sounded. The priests moved forward. The Lord whispered to Joshua, "Be strong and courageous. Obey all the law my servant Moses gave you. Do not turn from it to the right or to the left. No one will be able to stand against you. I will be with you. I will never leave you. You will be prosperous and successful, for the Lord your God will be with you wherever you go. Today I will exalt you in the eyes of all Israel, so they may know that I am with you as I was with Moses. Now, go. When you reach the edge of Jordan's waters, stand in the river."

Joshua waded into the river to await the Lord's power. Surely the people would know now if Joshua's words were true, if this man who followed in the sandals of Moses was truly a messenger from God.

When your time of testing comes, will you stand or be swept away? Will others follow or flee at the sound of your words? What will be the evidence of God's power in your life?

"We stand on the banks of the Jordan River," says Dr. Mark J. Chironna. "We are about to experience a generational shift, just as what had occurred with Moses and Joshua, and later with Elijah and Elisha. A generation rooted in warring for survival is passing off the scenes, and a generation more open and more capable of facing the future will emerge. Whether we use the metaphor of the Ark of the Covenant going before us, carried on the soft shoulders of priests, or the mantle of the prophet parting the waters, we stand on the threshold of a great transition. I believe we are about to experience a radical acceleration into the new and unexplored dimensions of Word and Spirit."

This new Promised Land, this rapid expansion and enlargement of God's Kingdom, belongs to those who are spiritually prepared, properly postured, and strategically positioned. Will you be ready?

Dr. Chironna is a second generation Italian American, born and raised in New York. Through his gifts of teaching he has spent much of his life discovering and developing strategies that deliver greater levels of healing, personal empowerment, and spiritual transformation. Trained as a theologian and certified personal coach, today he serves as a mentor, spiritual director, and physician of the soul.

"I've been walking with the Lord for 36 years. I had a radical conversion in December, 1973 and became totally redirected in terms of my life path and ministry. The best way I can describe my gift is that these pieces of information would pop into my spirit regarding people in a prayer meeting or room, and I would act on those hunches. There was just this awareness of things and people that I couldn't know by my own natural reasoning. No one had ever told me about the gifts of the Spirit, so I began to study the Word more systematically. Through this journey, I learned that what was working in me was the word of knowledge, the word of wisdom, and the gift of faith.

"What I lacked, though, was someone who could tell me about my gifts or how to use them. I learned about my gifting after the fact, and I honestly think that there are a lot of people today who are struggling like me. That's why I'm so excited about the growth and amplification of God's Kingdom. I truly believe some are standing on the banks of the Jordan and about to enter a new era."

As with all change, there will be those who long for the nostalgia of the past. Just as the people begged Elisha to find the departed Elijah, there will be some who cling to the old way, want to turn back and return to Egypt. This grieving is part of the growing process. We have to die to let go of 'what was' in order to live in the 'will be.'"

So how do we prepare ourselves to receive the gifts of the Spirit? What should our posture be as we embark on this new quest into His holy presence and power?

"It begins with strategic preparation," says Dr. Chironna. "Just as the offspring of Hebrew slaves had to prepare themselves to cross into the Promised Land, we too must prepare for God's provision. This preparation begins with cutting away the old self. In Joshua's day, this required a fresh circumcision. For Elisha, it was a sacrifice of everything he had worked for. Both metaphors represent a radical embrace of sacrifice and the crucified life. It is this cauterizing power of the Cross which releases the power of your spiritual gift."

As you move from slave, to self, to prophet with power, you may sense an inadequacy in your service.

"Using your spiritual gift can be both exciting and intimidating," Dr. Chironna explains, "because often you will find yourself doing things you'd never thought possible. I believe it's healthy to be uncomfortable with your gift because it is then, when you're uncomfortable, that you are totally dependent upon Him. Paul says, not that we are not adequate in ourselves, but our adequacy comes from God who makes us adequate vessels in Christ to minister in the Spirit." In other words, if you're not a little frightened by the raging waters, then you're probably not close enough to the river.

"For me," Dr. Chironna says, "this inner posture of inadequacy is an act of submission, a yielding to His leading. I know that without God's help and without God's power, nothing is going to happen. When I become aware that there are things going on that the Lord wants to address, that there are things I can't produce, manipulate, or manufacture on my own, then I know I'm walking in faith.

"The more you submit your work to God, the more accustomed you become to the process. In time, you'll become totally dependent on Him and learn, as Paul learned, that when you are weak, then you are strong. When you recognize that you are dead in Christ and that your life is hidden with Him, you can step out on faith and risk whatever you have for the sake of God's glory. And that's a healthy place to be.

"Even after 36 years of seeing God move, there are times when my knees still knock and my voice still trembles. On the one hand, I think this uncomfortable sense of walking by faith is a very healthy sign. It's our way of saying, 'Pay attention. You don't want to miss this.' On the other hand, you don't want to become bound so much by fear that you don't move at all.

"'Come here and listen to the words of the Lord your God," begins Joshua 3:9. "'This is how you will know that the living God is among you. ... See the ark of the covenant of the Lord of all the earth will go into the Jordan ahead of you.... So when the people broke camp to cross the Jordan, the priests carrying the Ark of the Covenant went ahead of them. Now the Jordan is at flood stage all during the harvest.'"

PREPARED, PURIFIED & OBEDIENT: THE PEOPLE OF GOD MOVE FORWARD IN FAITH

"It is here, in the posture of faith and humility, that you will find strategic portals, gateways, and places of access to change," Dr. Chironna says. "When we're yielded in faith, God moves. He confirms his word through signs and wonders. Yet as soon as the priests who carried the ark reached the Jordan, and their feet touched the water's edge, the water from upstream stopped flowing. It piled up in a heap a great distance away."

FAITH, SIGNS & WONDERS: THE MARKS OF A PROPHET MOVING IN GOD'S WILL

"When we stay in a posture of being little in our own eyes and move into a place of total confidence in God," Dr. Chironna concludes, "then we act in proportion to our faith. It is through preparation and posturing that we become aware of the promptings of the Spirit, of God placing us in position to do His work. Some of the discomfort we've felt in the past, the uneasiness of our own inadequacy, is overcome as we reflect on how God worked through us the last time.

"When we speak a word that's just the right word, when that utterance touches someone's need at just the right time, or when we get a sense that we need to pray for someone and that person gets healed, then we know were are responding to the promptings of the Holy Spirit and the gifts of the Holy Spirit."

Joshua watched as the priests carried the Ark of the Covenant into the waters. They stopped in the middle of the Jordan and stood on dry ground while all Israel passed before them. "Go over before the ark of the LORD your God into the middle of the Jordan. Each of you is to take up a stone on his shoulder, according to the number of the tribes of the Israelites, to serve as a sign among you. In the future, when your children ask you, 'What do these stones mean?' tell them that the flow of the Jordan was cut off before the Ark of the Covenant of the LORD. When it crossed the Jordan, the waters of the Jordan were cut off. These stones are to be a memorial to the people of Israel forever." (Joshua 4:5-7, NIV)

Preparation, posture, and position are the keys to prophetic utterances, faithful followers, and Superhuman Performance. To what new land, challenge, or mission is God calling you? Consecrate yourselves, for the Lord your God desires to do amazing things through you.

Gift Wrap:

- [The] new Promised Land, this rapid expansion and enlargement of God's Kingdom, belongs to those who are spiritually prepared, properly postured, and strategically positioned. Will you be ready?

- I believe it's healthy to be uncomfortable with your gift because it is then, when you're uncomfortable, that you are totally dependent upon Him.

- After 36 years of seeing God move, there are times when my knees still knock and my voice still trembles. On the one hand, I think this uncomfortable sense of walking by faith is a very healthy sign. It's our way of saying, 'Pay attention. You don't want to miss this.' On the other hand, you don't want to become bound so much by fear that you don't move at all.

Dr. Chironna's Other Gifts: Knowledge, Wisdom and Faith

CHAPTER 12

SECOND STRING STARTER

Roger Anderson: Act Righteously, Perform Remarkably

> Whatever you do, work at it with all your heart, as
> working for the Lord, not for human masters.
> —COLOSSIANS 3:23, NIV

Name: Roger Anderson
Position: President
Company: The Bob Pike Group
Spiritual Gifts: Leadership

"We've seen too many instances of greed and deception on Wall Street and in corporations," Roger Andersen says, "and because this was a topic with which I was deeply familiar, the Lord really brought it close to my heart, I grew up in a Christian family and went to a Christian evangelical college. Through my time in college, I had a lot of friends who became pastors and studied to go to the mission field, but I never felt called to do that. Instead, I got all excited about economics and business and was really pulled in that direction. But because I lacked a pastoral calling, I felt like I hadn't made the Lord's 'first team.'

"After graduation, I put all my energy into work and kind of shoved the Lord to the side. I had a successful career. But then about 15 to 20 years ago, I began to find my way back to God. When I became president of the last company, I sat down with my pastor and said, 'Joel, this time I really want to dedicate my job to the Lord. I want to honor Him with my work and glorify Him in everything that I do.'

"That was the first time in my career I really connected my work with my faith. Now at the same time, an executive on our company's board of directors was trying to get me to lie to auditors, deceive the bankers, and defraud our shareholders. It was all those things that you've read and seen on the news, only on a smaller scale. This wasn't the first time I'd faced this issue, though. Twice before I was fired because I wouldn't go along. Once I resigned rather than become mixed up in that sort of deception. So there I was again, facing corruption and being told to lie to my staff. I was advised to deceive potential buyers and exaggerate the value of our company so that we could make a lot of money. The stress was so bad that it drove me to my knees, and I said, 'Lord what do you want me to do?'

"He told me to quit. But how could I? I was 53 years old. What would I do next? He seemed to tell me, 'Those aren't the right questions to ask. Just obey me.' So I did.

"I spent about six months searching for what God wanted me to do next," Roger says. "Then one day after praying about my situation, I was in a bookstore and saw on the shelf this book called *Your Work Matters to God*. That night I read the book and everything just clicked. It was like the Lord was opening up Himself and answering my questions. I'd spent 30 years in the business world, and it all started to come together. The answer seemed simple. All I needed to do was honor the Lord in what I did. By just doing that, I could glorify Him.

"Over the next six months I ordered every book I could find on integrating faith and work. I read so deeply and took so many notes that one day I said to my wife, 'I think I know what the Lord wants me to do. I've got 50 to 70 pages of notes here. I think he wants me to write a book.' From those notes I wrote *The Executive Calling*. That book became a reflection of my own experiences and struggles of trying to integrate faith into my work. In there you'll find very practical tips and biblical guidance on succeeding in the corporate marketplace or the business marketplace and honoring God while doing it.

"For example, there is a ton of advice in Scripture about acting righteously. We're told not to lie, cheat, gossip, or hurt others. We're warned to not play politics and to refrain from backstabbing others. God's word gives us advice on how to care for our fellow workers. Really, it comes down to asking, 'How do I glorify God in my work?' After carefully reviewing the abundance of guidance and advice in Scripture, I think it boils down to two key principles: act righteously and perform remarkably."

But what does it mean to perform remarkably? We may hear about this less often in church, but I think it is just as important as acting righteously. It is the second part of the nature of God's work. God's work is righteous, and it is remarkable. In the early 1940s, there was a well-known English novelist, also a devout Christian, named Dorothy Sayers. Ms. Sayers made this observation in one of her speeches: 'No crooked table legs or ill-fitting drawers, I dare swear, came out of the carpenter's shop in Nazareth. Nor, if they had, could anyone believe they were made by the same hand that made heaven and earth.' Is it conceivable that Christ, during his young adult years as a carpenter, produced bad products? Do you think His customers were ever displeased with His workmanship?

What about the Apostle Paul? We know Paul largely supported himself as a tent and sail maker. Do you think Paul stitched crooked seams? Were his tents delivered on time? Were his sail repairs shoddy, his services fairly priced? If Paul's work proved inferior, then when he preached the gospel, his dissatisfied customers would have heckled him and called him a hypocrite. The quality of his craftsmanship was a direct reflection on the substance of God's good news.

"I'm confident that Paul was a good tent maker," Roger says. "In fact, I would bet that many of the people listening to Paul's testimony in the marketplace were customers who were first impressed by his good workmanship and honest commerce. Why is performing remarkably just as important as acting righteously? Because this is what makes people anxious to know more about us."

Tony Dungy, head coach of the Indianapolis Colts from 2002 to 2008, ran the team on Christian principles. Today, he is one of the most popular motivational speakers in the United States, drawing large crowds to hear his story, which always includes a testimony of faith in Jesus Christ. But these crowds want to hear him speak, not just because he acted righteously as a coach, but also because he performed remarkably. In 2007, his Colts won the Super Bowl.

"To perform remarkably is to fully use the gifts that God gave you," Roger adds. "Seek to discover the gifts that the Designer made in you, and pursue the work that best fits with those gifts so that you may perform as remarkably as possible. End each work day by taking an inventory of yourself. Ask yourself, 'Did I act righteously today? Did I perform remarkably?' You will know if you did or did not, and over time, as your answers become 'yes and yes,' you'll feel God's pleasure in your daily work."

"Occasionally I speak at Christian colleges in the midwest, and I usually end up talking to students who are in the business or economic schools. What I see in these Christians is the same thing that I went through when I was asking the Lord if it was okay for me to go into business. They'll say, 'You know, I feel like I am turning my back on the Lord by not following a calling to go into the ministry.' But as Christians, we need to stop thinking that way. God is in the marketplace. He created it. And He has gifted everyone in His own wisdom."

"Clergy are not the first stringers," Roger says. "God doesn't create second stringers and cast-offs from caregivers and managers and service industry employees who never received a call to the pulpit. As businessmen and women, we have a much larger opportunity to influence the world for Christ through our daily interactions. The clergy gets the 'saved' one day a week. Businesspeople have the chance to touch the 'unsaved' 24/7. He designed each of us equally, and He's got a purpose for all of us."

God designed all of us with unique gifts. God knows the very hairs on our head. He knew us before we were born. God specifically designed each of us, and He knew exactly how He designed us. God doesn't fill out his squad with benchwarmers. He has a purpose in His starting lineup for each of us.

"I love to explain to people that there is a tremendous need for Christians in leadership roles in the marketplace. All you have to do is pick up the newspaper and read about the corruption and greed. I would argue that there is a greater need for Christians in the marketplace than inside of the church. We can all go and hide in the church, but it's what we take out into the marketplace during the week that has a profound impact on God's Kingdom."

"This is important that He designed each of us for a unique purpose. It doesn't matter whether your gifts are to lead in great affairs or to serve well in small matters because each of us is placed by God in situations where we can reach others with the truth that saves. Paul wrote in 1 Corinthians 12:18 that, 'God has arranged the parts in the body, every one of them, just as he wanted them to be.' That means that none of us are insignificant in God's plan. The seemingly most insignificant person has just as important a role in God's kingdom as the leader of large organizations.

"Martin Luther King Jr. said it best: 'If a man is called to be a street sweeper, he should sweep streets even as Michelangelo painted, or Beethoven composed music, or Shakespeare wrote poetry. He should sweep streets so well that all the hosts of heaven and earth will pause to say, "Here lived a great street sweeper who did his job well."'"

"The first few chapters of Genesis provide a clear picture of one of God's greatest purposes for mankind. Scripture starts with, 'In the beginning God created...' and then in chapter two it says, '...so on the seventh day he rested from all his work.' Creation and work are used interchangeably and so the first attribute that we see of God is as a worker. Genesis 1:26 then says we are made in God's image, in the image of One who works. And finally God's purpose for us becomes clear in chapter two where we learn that the Lord put us in His creation to work. We are called to be God's co-workers in His creation! Work is given to us as a blessing. This is one key to finding your purpose. The very first and most important way in which we glorify God is by imitating Him in how we work.

"We're all called to be stewards of all God has entrusted to us," Roger says. "We're called to lead with integrity and serve the people placed in our care. But we're also called to be ambitious for the things of God. Ambition is mentioned five times in a negative way in the New Testament. And in each case, it's paired with the word 'selfish.' I would argue that if you have ambition to serve the Lord, then you should be open and eager to serve the Lord in the highest places that he can prepare you for. So, leadership and service are a powerful combination because people prefer to follow leaders who care about them and put them before themselves. We don't see that too often in the business world, but we could if more of God's people responded to His call to become ambassadors for Him in the marketplace."

The gift of leadership is the ability God gives to some people so they can shepherd others and act as effective stewards of the resources under His stewardship. Those with this gift are able to communicate clearly and inspire and encourage others to work harmoniously in accordance with God's purpose.

Everyone can be a leader. You don't need to be president of a company or even a department manager to be a leader. Each conversation we have with a person or within a group is an opportunity for leadership. Roger says that he often thinks of two principles related to leadership: servanthood and stewardship. The principle of servanthood is that the leader sees himself or herself as a servant to the people being led. We lead because we wish to have a positive impact on the people under our influence, not because of the gain or prestige that position and status brings us.

"The image of a shepherd is powerful," Roger says. "If you lead a group or an organization, picture the shepherd bringing the flock to a well. Does the shepherd drink first from the well and then go rest? Of course not. The shepherd first takes care of the flock, watering and feeding them before he takes care of his own needs. That is the image of a servant leader."

As servant leaders in a company, we treat others with respect and integrity. We motivate, set expectations, coach, and provide honest feedback because we pray for the success and growth of each person under our leadership.

"The good steward is another useful image. In biblical times, a steward was someone appointed to manage the household of a nobleman or wealthy merchant. Joseph was steward of Potiphar's household for a time. And we learn that from the time Joseph was put in charge, 'the blessing of the Lord was on everything that Potiphar had. In other words, Joseph's work resulted in prosperity for the owner.

"The two principles of stewardship are (1) we don't own anything, and (2) our master deserves a profitable return from our work. Money, titles, prestige, status, earthly possessions, they all perish; we don't own any of it. We're simply stewards for a time. Secondly, we each have gifts and talents, and the Lord expects us to use them profitably and to positively influence others. At the same time, our earthly masters expect a return from the responsibility they entrust to us. As president of a business, the owners or shareholders entrust me with their invested capital, the reputation of the business, the physical assets, and the human capital. As the steward for their business, my job is to meet expectations for growth and increase resources.

Gift Wrap:

- Leadership and service are a powerful combination because people prefer to follow leaders who care about them and put them before themselves. We don't see that too often in the business world, but we could if more of God's people responded to His call to become ambassadors for Him in the marketplace.

- As servant leaders in a company, we treat others with respect and integrity. We motivate, set expectations, coach, and provide honest feedback because we pray for the success and growth of each person under our leadership.

- "The two principles of stewardship are (1) we don't own anything, and (2) our master deserves a profitable return from our work.

Roger's Other Gift: Faith

CHAPTER 13

CHICK-FIL-A: WHERE BIBLICAL PRINCIPLES MAKE GOOD BUSINESS SENSE

Terry Butler: Feeding the Masses

And now, dear brothers and sisters, one final thing.
Fix your thoughts on what is true, and honorable,
and right, and pure, and lovely, and admirable. Think
about things that are excellent and worthy of praise.

—PHILIPPIANS 4:8, NIV

Name: Terry Butler
Position: Franchise Owner
Company: Chick-fil-A
Gift: Leadership

On a grass median encircling the main parking lot of a new
Chick-fil-A, college students mingle with corporate executives and construction workers. From a distance, camping
tents scattered atop black pavement appear as brightly colored

bubbles, awnings glistening as rain drops. Teens skip Frisbees off the sidewalk, angling to see who can launch their disks the farthest. In another corner of the lot, beach chairs mark the beginning of a line leading to the front door. These are manned by veterans, men and women of other grand openings. They arrived hours ago, some, even days ago. College students and part-time musicians, unemployed IT executives, and a women's book club, all were hoping to snag a free meal and more.

For almost a decade, the Chick-fil-A Corporation has celebrated each new restaurant by giving 52 chicken sandwich meal tickets (valued at $5.87) to each of the first 100 adults in line when doors open on the first day of business. A construction worker wearing a Chick-fil-A t-shirt and hat explains why he drove three hours to sit in the rain.

"First off, for the food. You can't beat their chicken sandwich. But these grand openings are also like a mini-vacation. Every time I come, I see folks from other openings, so it's like a reunion of sorts. And besides, where else can you spend a night camping out and get 52 meals for free?"

It's no coincidence that the crowd and the offer of free food invokes comparisons to a familiar Bible story where another mass of hungry followers gathered to be fed. For S. Truett Cathy, founder and chairman of Chick-fil-A, and his family, Christ's feeding of 5,000 people intersects nicely with the company's corporate values. While other restaurants remain open seven days a week, Chick-fil-A chooses to honor God by closing its doors on Sundays. Quirky and quaint, perhaps, but it's a business model that's reaped huge rewards. In fact, the firm's squeaky-clean reputation, loyalty to customers, and adherence to Christian values has made Chick-fil-A one of the top restaurants in the country, a legacy not lost on store owner Terry Butler.

> I don't get upset over things I can't control because if
> I can't control them, there's no use getting upset. And
> I don't get upset over the things I can control because
> if I can control them, there's no use in getting upset.
> —MICKEY RIVERS

"Working with the team at Chick-fil-A is not just a financial blessing but a spiritual one, too," Terry says. "I guess it was about five years ago that I was struggling with how to balance my spiritual gifts in the secular world. I was doing pretty well as a storeowner, but I was missing that sense of joy. A few days later, I was in a bookstore and happened to pick up Tom Newberry's book *The 4:8 Principle: The Secret to a Joy-Filled Life*. I read the first chapter in about 10 minutes, which is rare for me. Unless a book really grabs my interest, I usually put it down. But I ended up buying that book because Newberry talked about how life is meant to be full of joy, regardless of the circumstances. He went on to explain how we're to embrace our unique identity, that individualism can only be found in God.

"By the time I finished the book, I came to realize that joy is a journey, not a destination, and no matter where we are in our spiritual walk, as long as we have God, we can have joy because He is joy. He's love. He's truth. He's courage. He's abundant living. God is that and so much more. He is our provider, protection, honor, peace, rest, guide, Lord, sanctifier, and all those qualities we find in His character.

"Once I understood that, I discovered a liberty I'd never known before," Terry says. "I began to reorient my life toward seeking Him. As a result, I began to see that oftentimes, the thing you love to do is the thing God has called you to do. Not always, because He is God, and He can call us into some hard tasks. But, in general, I think he wants us to enjoy the fruit of our work. That's why I've become a big believer in doing what you love to do.

"When you view God's calling for your life in this light, your days don't seem like work. Instead, you find yourself saying, 'Wow! I get to do that?' So first, you need to understand that Christ came that we might have life and have it to the full. Not full as in wealth but fully living for Him."

"Second," Terry says, "you need to focus on the important things: family, friends, and most of all, your relationship with God. If you seek him daily, He will align your heart to His. In time, you'll find you desire the things He desires. When this happens, then it's easy to pray, 'Lord, your will be done,' because the thing He wants to do in your life is exactly the thing you want Him to do."

"Third, you need to surround yourself with people who share your beliefs," Terry says. "I call this building a hedge of protection. I'm not suggesting you assemble a bunch of yes-men and yes-women. On the contrary, having others with differing views is important to your growth and guidance. But your tribe should hold the same values as you, a similar love and faith in our Lord. These individuals will support you in your endeavors. They'll affirm your abilities, compliment you on your accomplishments, and serve as your guardrails when you stray from Him. If you don't have a tribe of loyal friends who will hold you accountable, it's going to be a very difficult for you to be successful. Whether it's a friend, spouse, or family member, you need that outer strength to hold you tight.

"As the owner of a franchise restaurant, I learned long ago that it pays to be loyal to my employees. That's why we're called a team and not a staff. The other thing we have is what I call 'the mother effect.' You really want to make sure you treat everybody like you want your momma treated. That's just the bottom line. If you really wrap yourselves around that concept and don't view customers as clients but as family, then you begin to see each day as a joyful experience and not work. That is, after all, one of our main purposes here on earth, to serve others and love God. Do those three things —live abundantly in Him, focus on the important things, and serve others —and success will follow."

"Now for me," Terry says, "all of this is bathed in hope. I'm probably the most optimistic person you'll ever meet. If we're playing ball and my team is down 20 to nothing with 10 seconds left, I still think we can win the game. So for me, hope and optimism have never been an issue. I just look at things on the bright side and figure God is in control.

"After all, why should we spend our time worrying about things we can't change? That's why I try to motivate my team to focus on the things within their reach, to find a way to make an impact in the small world around them. If each of us will do that, then the ripples will rush outward, creating a positive effect in our community. I say, control what you have control over, and don't worry about those circumstances you can't control because if you do, they'll control you."

"All successful businessmen and women are good listeners. And yet this is one of the easiest and least used skills. We've become so busy and distracted that we don't have time to deeply hear what others are saying, which is a shame because a lot of times, those around us are crying out for help, begging for someone to notice them. If you want to gain insight into how to touch the wounds of others, then learn to listen. Do that and you'll be surprised how many new friends you make."

"Finally, I believe in making friends wherever I go. I believe if you make friends, you have fewer enemies. But if you want to test this theory, just stand inside a crowded elevator and look everyone in the eye and smile. Say 'hello.' Sure, you'll get some strange looks. But you'll also connect and bring a smile to someone who might otherwise have been experiencing a bad day. That one small gesture could become the seed of a relationship and change a person's day. People gravitate towards those who make them feel welcome, recognized, honored, and valued. I mean, isn't that part of what attracts us to a relationship with Christ? Even though we're flawed, He welcomes us as we are. For me, that's part of The Great Commission, to relate to those God places along our path. That, and serve great chicken."

Gift Wrap:

- Focus on the important things: family, friends, and most of all, your relationship with God.

- If you don't have a tribe of loyal friends who will hold you accountable, it's going to be a very difficult for you to be successful."

- You really want to make sure you treat everybody like you want your momma treated.

- Control what you have control over, and don't worry about those circumstances you can't control because if you do, they'll control you.

Terry's Other Gifts: Faith

CHAPTER 14

GOD SPECIALIZES IN ORIGINALS

Keith Harrell: Attitude is Everything

And Moses said unto the LORD, 'O my LORD, I am
not eloquent, neither heretofore, nor since thou hast
spoken unto thy servant: but I am slow of speech,
and of a slow tongue.'

—EXODUS 4:10, KJV

> **Name**: Keith Harrell (Deceased)
> **Position**: Speaker, Consultant & Author
> **Company**: Harrell Performance Systems, Inc.
> **Gift**: Encouragement

Lean, lanky, and shy, Keith Harrell squirmed in his seat as the kindergarten teacher reviewed her class roster. He knew it would begin: the taunting and teasing, the endless jokes. He'd hoped the other kids would go easy on him, give him a few days to settle in before picking on him. But they pounced as soon as they had learned he was different.

The catcalls had begun on the steps of the school and had followed him down the hall until, at last, he had escaped into his classroom.

Now he stood before the others, hands sweating, lip quivering. His teacher looked up from the roster, waiting. Opening his mouth, Keith formed half a consonant, half the hard *keh* of *Keith*, but that was all he could say.

The girl next to him snickered. Others followed. At recess, Keith bolted from the school, vowing never to go back, promising himself he'd never present himself as a spectacle or be ridiculed again. But in the years to follow, Keith would learn how an all-powerful God can take a blubbering kindergartner and transform him into a mighty man.

> A smooth sea never made a skilled mariner.
> —ENGLISH PROVERB

"That first day of school, my teacher asked all the kids to stand up and say their names," says Keith. "When it was my turn, I rose from my chair and stuttered so much I couldn't even finish. The other kids began laughing. Even today, I can still hear their giggles. I lived two miles away, and as soon as I had the chance, I ran home as fast as I could. I remember running up the steps and onto our front porch and Mom coming out of the house and giving me a big hug. When I tried to explain what had happened, she said she already knew. My teacher had called. 'Honey, I know this hurts,' Mom said, 'but we're not going to worry. We're going to work hard. Mommy's going to get you some help because Mommy can already see it. And you need to start seeing it, too. You need to start seeing that one day you're going to stand tall. One day you're going to say your name as loud and as well as all the other boys and girls.'

"As it turns out, Mom was right. God specializes in originals, restorations, and repairs."

> It is difficult to say what is impossible, for the dream of yesterday is the hope of today and the reality of tomorrow.
>
> —ROBERT H. GODDARD

> Don't be afraid to give your best to what seemingly are small jobs. Every time you conquer one, it makes you that much stronger. If you do the little jobs well, the big ones will tend to take care of themselves.
>
> —DALE CARNEGIE

Now a highly successful speaker, author, and consultant, Keith specializes in helping others move past their temporary limitations and toward the unique individual God meant for them to become.

"I like to ask people, 'So what's bugging you?' because we're all bugged by something. We're bugged by people, problems, and plans that fall through. Over my lifetime I have found that your attitude controls your altitude. To a large extent, what you think you can do will determine how far and high you fly.

"Years ago, I was sitting in a packed room with about 650 other employees when the marketing director came in. Speaking in a very deep voice to a hushed room, he announced that my company, IBM, was about to lay off 40,000 people.

'I'm sorry to be the bearer of bad news,' he explained, 'but 80 percent of you won't be here in three months.' I watched as attitudes went from an all time high to a basement-level low in a matter of seconds. Jumping from my chair, I said 'I have a question. Can I have a bigger office? One with a window view?' I thank my Lord and Savior Jesus Christ for allowing me to speak boldly and turn a very stressful situation into one of hope. Looking back, I believe God put me in a place right then to do exactly what he predestined me to do, which is to be an encourager to others, to help them through challenging times. So, when I speak of projecting a positive attitude, this is what I mean: Don't assume the negative. Expect the positive."

But embracing his gift as an encourager wasn't always easy for Keith. His growth in encouragement took time, years of discernment, and hard work as he removed the clutter from his life.

"My gift didn't become clear to me until I started tithing," Keith says. "I'd worked at IBM for 14 years and never once had I tithed. But, after I left the company and started my own business, I was placed in a position where I had to rely on God. I had so much fear in me that I said, 'I've got to do the things I know God wants me to do.' And one of those things was tithing. I think that's what He wanted to reveal to me, that in order to truly use your gift and serve Him, you have to line up your actions with His word and commands. Once you tap into His ways, then the God-given abilities you already have come forth.

"After I began tithing and trusting God, I was able to grow my own business. Before, I'd had the confidence but not the faith to succeed. Then, the Lord led me to a couple of resources, mentors who could help guide me to where God was leading. You know, it's only through God's grace and through the support of people like Les Brown and others that I was able to get up and keep moving. That's what we need, a support group that will help us up when we've been knocked down. I think one of the keys to using your spiritual gifts to perform at extraordinary levels is to surround yourself with the right people, people who will help you stay under the power of prayer and in the center of God's will. Les also encouraged me to start going to church and reading my Bible. When I did that, I began renewing my mind with the word of God and was able to build my business to the level it is today."

"First," Keith says, "I would say you need to make an appraisal of your skills, knowledge, and experience. When I was at IBM, I was in sales. They came to me and asked if I'd become a sales trainer. Well, that was something I didn't want to do because, again, fear was knocking at the door. But, when I finally got into that position and started seeking out other coaches, other people that were already doing well in that capacity, my passion for sharing the knowledge I had and my desire to help others allowed me to excel. So, I say if you have a gift to speak, train, or teach, then seek out a mentor or a coach, someone who's already doing those things, and then get close to them."

Remove the Rocks From Your Path

> Our decision to close on Sundays honors God. It
> also helps us attract the caliber of employees who
> appreciate having Sundays off.
>
> —S. TRUETT CATHY

"With the right attitude, you can turn a setback into stepping stones," Keith says, "provided you don't allow yourself to believe that your situation is permanent. A setback means an unanticipated delay or reverse in progress, an unfortunate happening that hinders or impedes. The key word is *hinder*. It means something has inserted itself between you and your destination. Without life's ups and downs and the temporary joys and defeats, you would never know the stock you are made of. So allow yourself the time to learn the lessons derived from your setback. Then, use that setback as the stepping stone for the next big thing God has planned for you."

Maintain a Positive Attitude

What is it that you've always wanted to do? People with a positive attitude are influenced by what goes on within them. People with a negative attitude are influenced by what goes on around them. Your attitude determines whether you're living life or life's living you, whether you're on the way or in the way. See your setback as an opportunity to pursue your heart's desire, that one thing God has placed on your heart.

> And it is a good thing to receive wealth from God
> and the good health to enjoy it. To enjoy your work

and accept your lot in life —this is indeed a gift
from God.
—ECCLESIASTES 5:19, NLT|

Get busy setting goals, learning the skills you'll need for the
small tasks, networking with others in your new field, attending
conferences, speaking from your area of expertise, and defining
the shape of your destiny. If God has placed this desire in your
heart, then it's His work, not yours, but He needs your sweat to
bring it to completion.

To a large extent, you determine if the seeds you scatter,
grow. If you allow setbacks to overwhelm and overcome you,
the seeds will shrivel up and die. However, if you quit complaining about what has happened and, instead, constantly affirm
your gifts and talents and hustle to reach your goal, you'll overcome any situation that tries to hold you back.

"Finally, determine what price you are willing to pay for
your gift," says Keith. "A lot of times a gift may be just a hobby.
It doesn't have to be a career or a calling. It could be something
you enjoy doing. Your gifting may not mean that's going to be
your destiny. But, if it is your calling and purpose, know in
advance that it's going to exact a cost.

"The closer you get to your gift, the more you see what's
required in terms of talent, preparation, and education. Ask
yourself, 'Do I have a natural ability in this area? Am I willing
to work at the craft? How hard is it going to be for me to be not
just good, but great? Am I prepared to pay that price?'

"You know a lot of people say they want to perform at the
highest level," Keith says, "but it's another thing to see all that

goes into reaching that pinnacle of perfection. I recommend you seek out those individuals who have already paid their price, struggled, overcome, and built their spiritual muscles. Then you'll know if you're committed, allowing the Holy Spirit to use you for God's work. And if not, if the task seems too daunting right now, then pray that God will change your heart and give you the strength to move forward. That is what going the extra mile for Christ is all about."

> Joy is an outward sign of inward faith in the promises of God.
>
> —TOMMY NEWBERRY

Gift Wrap:

- I think one of the keys to using your spiritual gifts to perform at extraordinary levels is to surround yourself with the right people, people who will help you stay under the power of prayer and in the center of God's will.

- If you have a gift to speak, train, or teach, then seek out a mentor or a coach, someone who's already doing those things, and then get close to them.

- With the right attitude, you can turn a setback into stepping stones.

- Your attitude determines whether you're living life or life's living you, whether you're on the way or in the way. See your setback as an opportunity to pursue your heart's desire, that one thing God has placed on your heart.

I see no conflict between biblical principles and good business practice.

—S. Truett Cathy

Keith's Other Gifts: Giving

PROCLAIMING THE LORD'S FAVOR

Alma Rivera: Tú Mereces Gloria

The *pop, pop, pop* of gunfire sent pedestrians scurrying for cover behind trucks and sedans parked along a crowded street in Reynosa, Mexico. The grocer hurried inside his shop and hid behind the counter, waiting, listening for the return of gunfire. Peeking above the counter, he looked through the front window of his store and across the street. Two men stood inside the lobby of a stucco building. Another knelt between them. *Pop!*

The man on his knees fell forward.

Moments later, two youths dragged the body of a police officer outside, dumping him by the curb. One of the men spoke into a handheld radio, pausing to listen to the crackled voice coming from the speaker. Nudging the body off the curb and onto a drainage grate, the two youths climbed into the cab of an olive-green truck and pulled away.

When he was certain the pair was gone, the grocer ran outside to join the crowd who'd gathered around the slain officer. Some people wept, others spit. The grocer looked down at his friend and shook his head. When would the killing stop? Each day there were more of them, more narco-traffickers. They'd roamed his streets, killing his customers, beheading policemen. The day before, he'd watched them gun down a bodyguard outside a gated home. He did not want to stay in Reynosa, but what choice did he have? He could not move to America and leave his family and business. No, he would stay and pray for help. Perhaps God would hear. Maybe He would show favor on Reynosa and send someone to help, send someone who would change the hearts of the evil men.

Alma Rivera was born in Mexico City, Mexico. At the age of 11, she accepted Jesus as her Lord and Savior, but it wasn't until almost ten years later, while at the Biblical Institute of World Ministries in Morelia, Mexico, that Alma sensed God calling her to serve Him through singing.

"In 2002 I was living in Reynosa, Mexico," she says. "I'd been a musician and singer for about six years when one morning I awoke with this dream in my head. It was so clear. I felt God had told me to start a worship school. I saw a school, students —everything. And I was completely in shock because obviously I didn't have teachers or instruments. But then God gave me the passage from John 4:24 that says, 'God is spirit, and his worshipers must worship in the Spirit and in truth.' I believed this was what He wanted me to do, so even though I didn't have any students, I began to walk by faith, asking, 'Okay, Lord. How will I do this?'

"In Reynosa, I found this building for rent. I told the lady who was there, 'Listen, I want to start a school here.' When I told her I wanted to start a worship school, she was so excited; she was a Christian too. 'When do you plan to start this school?' the woman asked."

"I told her in March and that I had no students. She said the sweetest thing: 'You know, Alma, I like you. And I know God will provide everything you need for your worship school.' Turning to her daughter, she said, 'Take down the advertisement. This building is now rented.'"

"Now I thought when we opened we might have 15 or 20 students," Alma says, "but around 200 people came to our worship school. I was shocked! Everybody was looking at me, the teachers, the students. I had brought them there thinking we would start small. When they asked what we were going to do, I told them, 'I don't know, but God does.' And so we went to work doing what we could, where we were, with what we had.

"Today we have around 100 students in the school, which shows you how much God's hand was in the project. But it's not a worship school that trains you to be a musician. It helps you become a worshiper because praising Him includes anointing and excellence.

"There is a lot of crime in Reynosa. It is a very dangerous place. But I was so tired of the violence that I told my students we needed to do something. We couldn't just learn and not give back.

"So we started performing outside and doing evangelistic concerts in the middle of the plaza. Then we opened our school to unsaved people because that allowed us to tell them about Jesus. The mayor thought we were crazy, but we were saving people through music. God blessed us a lot in that time in Reynosa, but that project would never have happened without God's hand blessing me.

"You see, when I was around 15, I received a call from God. He was speaking to me from Isaiah 61:1-2 where it says, 'The Spirit of the Sovereign Lord is on me because the Lord has anointed me to proclaim good news to the poor.'

"I knew I would do this through singing," Alma says, "because I believe when I sing, I'm using my gift to bring deliverance and give healing. My music is for building up other people's faith. But, there are those times when the enemy will test to see who you are in God. He wants to see if we are Sunday Christians or Christians who walk in the authority that they have been given by God.

"That's what happened with me. I was worshiping Him one day when I developed a sore throat. The doctor gave me this kind of medicine. It was for asthma or something. Every day I was putting this on my throat. And all of a sudden, this medicine damaged my vocal cords. I couldn't sing for a year. When I tried to talk, it was like I was whispering."

"Do you know what it's like to have a gift and not be able to us use it? You feel dead. Because I wanted to use my singing to honor the Lord and minister to people but couldn't, I continued to pray and worship. But I did it without a voice."

"The thing I learned, though, is that you don't need to be a good singer to worship. It didn't matter how good I sounded.

So, I'd just be in my bedroom worshiping Him with my bad voice ruined by this attack from the enemy, and I'd be whispering, 'Lord I need you' because I couldn't sing or speak loud enough to say it.

"And God heard me. Even in my broken whisper, He heard me. I know, because around that time someone called me about an event at church. I told the person I couldn't sing, that my voice was gone. But I went anyway because, like I said, praising Him doesn't require perfection, only obedience.

"I was on the platform with all these musicians and singers, and I looked at the people in the audience. Then the music started. I opened my mouth and all of sudden I started to sing. It was a miracle. I looked to the worship leader, and he saw that I was singing so he called me in front, and I just kept singing. I didn't know if I'd ever sing again, but at that moment, I was singing. And I was praising God because He'd released a miracle in my life."

How can others perform at superhuman levels using the spiritual gifts God gives them? Alma says you must be anointed by God, persistent through trials, and pure of heart.

Gift Wrap

- You can't just grab a gift and try to use it to be popular or famous or get money. If you do, you'll get crushed.

- It's very difficult to become successful using your gift if God hasn't anointed you for that work.

- God will connect you with the right people and lead you to success in the things that matter to Him.

Alma's Other Gifts: Faith

APPENDIX: RELATED READING

ADMINISTRATION

1 Corinthians 12:28-31
Luke 14:28-30

CRAFTSMANSHIP

Exodus 28:3-4
Exodus 31:1-11
Exodus 35:30-35

DISCERNMENT

1 Corinthians 12:7-11
1 John 4:1-6
1 Corinthians 2:9-16
2 Chronicles 2:12
Psalms 119:125
Proverbs 3:21
1 Kings 3:9
Hebrews 5:14

FAITH

1 Corinthians 12:7-11
Mark 5:25-34

Acts 27:21-25

Hebrews 11

Romans 4:18-21

GIVING

Romans 12:6-8

2 Corinthians 9:6-15

2 Corinthians 8:2-5

Mark 12:41-44

Matthew 6:3-4

KNOWLEDGE

And by knowledge shall the chambers be filled with all precious and pleasant riches.

—PROVERBS 24:4

For the transgression of a land many are the princes thereof, but by a man of understanding and knowledge the state thereof shall be prolonged.

—PROVERBS 28:2

For the LORD gives wisdom; from His mouth come knowledge and understanding.

—PROVERBS 2:6

The mind of the prudent acquires knowledge, And the ear of the wise seeks knowledge.

—PROVERBS 18:15

> My people are destroyed for lack of knowledge: because thou hast rejected knowledge, I will also reject thee, that thou shalt be no priest to me: seeing thou hast forgotten the law of thy God, I will also forget thy children.
>
> —Hosea 4:6

WRITING

1 Tim. 3:14-15—As I write this letter to you, I hope to come and see you soon. But if I delay, this letter will let you know how we should conduct ourselves in God's household, which is the church of the living God, the pillar and support of the truth.

John 20:30-31—In his disciples' presence Jesus performed many other miracles which are not written down in this book. But these have been written in order that you may believe that Jesus is the Messiah, the Son of God, and that through your faith in him you may have life.

1 John 2:12-14—I write to you, my children, because your sins are forgiven for the sake of Christ. I write to you, fathers, because you know him who has existed from the beginning. I write to you, young men, because you have defeated the Evil One. I write to you, my children, because you know the Father. I write to you, fathers, because you know him who has existed from the beginning. I write to you, young men, because you are string; the word of God lives in you, and you have defeated the Evil One.

Jude 1:3—Dear friends, although I was very eager to write to you about the salvation we share, I felt compelled to write and urge you to contend for the faith that was once for all entrusted to God's holy people.

1 Timothy 3:14-15—Although I hope to come to you soon, I am writing you these instructions so that, if I am delayed, you will know how people ought to conduct themselves in God's household, which is the church of the living God, the pillar and foundation of the truth.

MUSIC

1 Samuel 16:14-23
1 Corinthians 14:26
Psalm 33:1-3
Psalm 96:1-2
Psalm 100:1-2
Psalm 149:3
Psalm 150:1-6
Colossians 3:16
2 Chronicles 5:12-13
2 Samuel 6:14-1

BIBLIOGRAPHY:

The Gallup Organization *Building a Highly Engaged Workforce: How great managers inspire virtuoso performance.* Princeton, NJ: Gallup Poll 2002.

Adelaja, Sunday. *Money Won't Make Your Rich: God's Principles for True Wealth, Prosperity, and Success.* Kiev, Ukraine: Charisma House, 2009.

Blackaby, Henry. *Experiencing God: Knowing and Doing the Will of God.* Atlanta, GA: Broadman and Holman, 2008.

Foreman, George. *Knockout Entrepreneur: My Ten Count Strategy For Winning at Business.* Houston, TX: Thomas Nelson, 2009.

Barna, George. Survey Describes the Spiritual Gifts That Christians Say They Have. Ventura, CA: Barna Group 2001.

THE MILESTONE BRAND

Free Gift Assessment: Learn Your Gift Today!

www.milestonebrand.com

7413 Six Forks Road

Suite 301

Raleigh, NC 27615

info@milestonebrand.com

ABOUT THE AUTHORS

Darrayl Miles is the Senior Vice President of The Milestone Brand, an insurance executive and a professional actor. Despite his hectic schedule, Darrayl aggressively finds time to enjoy his wife Twarnette. They have four children between them and reside in Central Florida.

Derrick Miles is the Chairman/CEO of The Milestone Brand and a corporate operations improvement consultant. He was a senior executive with operational responsibilities for several healthcare corporations prior to developing the Superhuman Performance® franchise. Derrick and his wife Michele have two children. They reside in the Triangle of North Carolina.